I0644690

the selected poems of steve dalachinsky

Advance Praise for *The Selected Poems of Steve Dalachinsky*

"Steve Dalachinsky not only wrote poetry, he lived and breathed it. From his music poems to haiku to New York poems, this captivating collection is a testament of a life steeped in poetry and a devotion to all art forms and expression. Each poem reverberates a voice of incomparable depth, rawness, and honesty."

—**MARISOL LIMÓN MARTÍNEZ**, AUTHOR OF *VIA DISSIMULATA*

"Dalachinsky is New York City's greatest *poète maudit*, only he threw off the curse of madness & embraced the excesses & singularity of free jazz as well as art, low, high, & everywhere in between to create a body of work that dovetails closely with his fellow travelers Amiri Baraka, Ted Joans, & the irreducible Ornette Coleman. A poetry of sensation merging with cosmic ideas spilling from these pages onto your hands, Dalachinsky's poems are an essential handbook of what it is like to seek the sacred song of jazz in the embarcadero night while hawking records on the street by day & sweeping the steps by grey morning light. Steve's oeuvre connects us back to the Beats & the mystic revelations of William Blake."

—**JEFFREY JOE NELSON**, AUTHOR OF *ROAD OF A THOUSAND WONDERS*

"Every word in this book is alive with Dalachinsky's grouchy-tender vulnerability. Nothing could be as good as looking into his eyes and hearing his voice again, but this book comes close."

—**JULIEN POIRIER**, AUTHOR OF *OUT OF PRINT*

"In my way of seeing it, Steve doesn't fit into any neat category, academic or otherwise. And being an autodidact, his reality and art are a homemade reality and art. Steve in a certain way was always working on his language—taking impressions from all manner of phenomenon and mutating and fracturing that into his verse—and a lot of the pieces might have been spontaneous, but there was a method that was constantly refining itself and allowed him to create verse like that. Take each poem as it is; maybe Steve is beyond category."

—**MATTHEW SHIPP**, FREE-JAZZ PIANIST AND AUTHOR OF *BLACK MYSTERY PIANISTS AND OTHER WRITINGS*

"Who better writes about the 'i' than Dalachinsky? He examines, interrogates, accuses, pronounces, forgives, empathizes, and laughs at the self via the poem. The love poems are confessionals. The dexterity in the way he changes pace, rhythm, and pitch on the page is like Bird changing keys during a solo. Nobody can employ a refrain to hypnotize like Steve Dalachinsky."

—**TATE SWINDELL**, AUTHOR OF *SOLAR HITS*

the selected poems of steve dalachinsky

edited by Michael Ruby and Yuko Otomo

city lights / san francisco

Cover art by Steve Dalachinsky, *New York Trilogy #2* (2013), paper collage on cardboard

Cover design by Jeff Mellin
Text design by Patrick Barber

The interior collages by Steve Dalachinsky were made in 2010 for an unrealized book of collages called *Bug Anthology*.

ISBN 978-0-87286-924-0

Library of Congress Cataloging-in-Publication Data

Names: Dalachinsky, Steven author | Otomo, Yuko editor | Ruby, Michael (Michael Handler) editor
Title: The selected poems of Steve Dalachinsky / edited by Michael Ruby and Yuko Otomo.
Description: San Francisco : City Lights, 2026.
Identifiers: LCCN 2026013789 (print) | LCCN 2026013790 (ebook) | ISBN 9780872869240 paperback | ISBN 9780872869769 ebook
Subjects: LCGFT: Poetry
Classification: LCC PS3554.A41465 S45 2026 (print) | LCC PS3554.A41465 (ebook) | DDC 811/.54—dc23/eng/20260406
LC record available at https://lccn.loc.gov/2026013789
LC ebook record available at https://lccn.loc.gov/2026013790

City Lights Books are published at the City Lights Bookstore,
261 Columbus Avenue, San Francisco, CA 94133
www.citylights.com

i've always had a deathwish
but within that wish was the notion
i'd live forever

it's difficult
to imagine the world
without me
yet on the other hand
it's quite a
relief

— s.d.

table of contents

II. NEW YORK POEMS

III. HAIKU

IV. MUSIC POEMS

V. FRENCH POEMS

VI. LATER POEMS

FOREWORD

FOREWORD

Yuko Otomo

Before I start the "Who/What/How" about the author of this book, the inimitable, one and only Steve Dalachinsky, I need to make one thing clear for the record. Although it is posthumously completed, this book was *not* a posthumous project. Its genesis goes back to the time when Steve was still with us. It all started with the friendship between Steve and Michael Ruby, who is co-editing this book with me.

They first met at a book launch party held at Michael's house in Brooklyn in 2010. Their friendship quickly flourished because of their shared love for poetry and music. In March 2015, Michael suggested it was time for Steve to do a "collected works" project. In response, Steve said to him, "*Collected Works*!?! That's impossible! It'll be more than 10 Volumes! You know I've been crazy writing so much ever since I was a kid!" True: Steve was one of the most obsessively prolific writers you can imagine. So they both agreed to settle for *Selected Poems*. They got together often to create the basic structure of the book. Michael also conducted an immensely detailed interview with him going back to Steve's earliest memories. By the summer of 2019, they had almost finished formatting the table of contents. Then, BANG! Steve suddenly collapsed after an intense reading and passed away in early fall of 2019, to our utmost sadness. So, naturally, the project was paused.

After the overwhelming, unbearable pain and sorrow of losing so suddenly the love of my life, a life I shared with him so intimately over four decades, I woke up one day and determined to take over Steve's role as the co-editor, to help keep my sanity intact. During the prolonged isolation of the pandemic, in my solitude, I delved into the project further, going through his writing from early childhood to the present, page by page, poem by poem. I was mesmerized with the vastness and the depth of his world as I went through his oeuvre. It was like knowing him again with an astute focus, strictly through the lens of poetry. I got obsessively involved in the process, which gave me such a rich and empowering spirit to survive the hardest time of my life. Michael was very pleased with my assuming the role of co-editor, and we corresponded frequently over the project.

Here, I'd like to take the opportunity to express my gratitude to Michael, who initiated this whole chain of events. With his insightful conviction regarding the importance of Steve and his writing, with a deeply historical understanding, through his unshakable selfless devotion to the project, he led Steve and then myself on this path to complete this book. Without his clearheaded leadership, this book could have never come to life. He planted the seed of thought in us and kept nurturing it with focused efforts and involvement, encouraging us steadily to go on, and to finally reach its completion. Thank You, Michael. Words are never sufficient enough here to express our deep appreciation.

❁

Born in 1946, a postwar baby in Brooklyn, NY, Steve was a New Yorker through and through, spending most of his adult life in Downtown NYC. He was a human dynamo, always expanding and experimenting in many directions, with a limitless rigor that rejected narrow-scoped, easy categorization or labeling of any kind. He was a quintessential *organic intellectual* in Antonio Gramsci's definition. He was a grand master autodidact with no institutional degrees. He was an outsider/outcast, a rebel, a bohemian, a superintendent, a street vendor, the best secondhand clothes dresser, a hypersensitive insomniac, and more. He knew how to talk to cats and dogs and newborn babies, or to a stranger whom he just met. He was a lover and a friend to anyone and anything. He was *a Boomer with a cause*.

A polymath, he had limitless, boundless curiosities and hunger for everything. He was a poet, a collagist, a *hai-jin* (haiku writer), a music lover, a (free) jazz aficionado, a music critic, a liner-notes writer, a performance poet collaborating with musicians here and abroad, a visual art enthusiast, a mail artist, a devoted cineaste, an avid record/book collector, a newspaper columnist, a doo-wop singer, etc. For me, he was a lover, a husband, the best supporter of my creative life, a partner in crime excavating and exploring the world of creativity and beyond. We were like the two characters Estragon (Gogo) and Vladimir (Didi), in Beckett's play *Waiting for Godot*. It almost makes me dizzy to remember his life in its detailed expansions and descriptions. But no matter what role he played or what situation he was in, he was (as our close friend, the late, great pianist Cecil Taylor, used to call him, using this title instead of his first name) a poet, through and through, all in all. He was a *genus irritabile* and a quintessential *poète maudit*. He was almost always overwhelmed by his own *joie de vivre*. Till the last moment, he chased the joy of life to the maximum. Although it took a while for him to publicly accept the general designation "poet" (which he took very seriously) to explain who/what he was, he was clearly aware of the cosmic role given to him in this universe since an early age. It was heartbreakingly moving to go through the pages of his early notebooks, preciously kept and saved by him, to feel his naïve but pure and noble self-awareness of his vocation. As for the influences on his creative life and beyond, he often talked of jazz, Homer's *Odyssey*, Blake, Lorca, e. e. cummings, Beat Generation writers, haiku, especially Issa, Dadaism, Surrealism, Cubism, Pataphysics, Existentialism, and other avant-garde art movements. Essentially, he was a Romantic by nature. He believed in love and friendship as he believed in art and creativity. Every moment of his life—24/7,

365 days a year, all the way until he departed—was consumed more than 100% with these principal beliefs.

As the natural part of his *poète maudit* persona, his life was not easy. Living in an old tenement shoebox apartment, he did not have a study with a desk and a chair or any other comfortable environment to compose his poetry or create his art/collages or a social position to present them to the public. He wrote standing, walking, listening, talking, sitting in buses and on the train, in music venues, in museums, in galleries and in cafés, contemplating reality and dreams; he made art on the kitchen table, sharing it with me. He always carried pieces of scrap paper and a few pens (in case one ran out of ink) in his shirt or jacket pocket and wrote whenever and wherever the poetic inspiration hit him. In order to share his creation, to deliver his words to the world, he read in any and every possible space, such as community gardens, libraries, parks, bookstores, record stores, schools, private salons, weddings, memorials, bars, restaurants, and even the streets. His works were published mainly by small presses, journals, periodicals, and magazines, occasionally even in some academic venues, as he had no hierarchical judgments or prejudices over social capital status or values. He wanted to reach out to unknown readers as much as possible, disregarding all the hardships. He talked of his creative process as the transformative poetic alchemical merging of the internals and externals of the life he breathed. He was a filter, a mediator, and a furnace of the moment.

He had a deep-seated, clear, austere sense of personal responsibility of his role as a poet throughout his life, although he shied away from its public image. Every night after coming home from the long night's excursion following music and fun, he never failed to rewrite poems he scribbled on pieces of paper down neatly into a notebook in the early days, or later typed them up on the computer with the date and the title (if any). He was a fierce believer in improvisational intuitive spirits, so he rarely edited his works. It is fascinating to see how his original, scribbled handwriting shows all the internal poetic process of creation as if the spirit dictated them! Through his dedicated efforts, they found resting places in the notebooks and on the computer, saved to share with others. What a blessing it is that he left a big treasure box full of poems, breathing their original spirit for us to tap into, to enjoy his magical world. I thank him for having such a devoted manner of keeping his creations in an organized chronology, which made our job as editors smooth and easy. It was truly a mesmerizing and rewarding experience and a special privilege to go through his archived materials one by one from his childhood writing to the last poem he wrote, only two days before his passing. It was like walking a poet's path again together with him to trace life's richness filled with light, shadow, color, and music.

The hardest part was to do the selection from the uncountably huge amounts of work left by him. He literally wrote hundreds of poems! As Michael half-jokingly said, "It would be so much easier to do the *Collected Works*!" Totally true. It could have been so much easier for us to have all the poems he wrote since he was young to fill the pages of volume after volume. Indeed, it was a heart-wrenchingly painful process to go through them, keeping some *in* and leaving some *out*. In order to ease our struggle over the hardship, we kept encouraging each other, saying "Let's not worry about that too much right now! One day, we'll do the *Collected Works*!"

Here you are! We did our best at presenting works from every aspect of Who/What/How he was to show the whole scope of his being. Yet, no matter how hard we tried, this book is still an introductory effort. We selected a sampling of his work to guide and to invite the readers to open the doors into his poetic world. We tried to choose each poem with the simplest categorical flow. Many publications from City Lights were essential sources of intellectual and creative nutrients and inspiration that Steve enjoyed over many years, not just for his role as a poet but also for the enrichment of his overall human existence. I am sure that he is happy, smiling from the above, looking at this beautiful City Lights edition of his *own* book. He'd be so proud of joining the family of the heroes he loved, adored, and respected. It is like a dream come true for him and for us as well to give birth to this book. I'd love to thank our longtime friends Julien Poirier and Tate Swindell for their loving support and Garrett Caples and Elaine Katzenberger of City Lights for embracing the idea of publishing Steve's work with wholehearted openness. Michael and I were extremely blessed with the collective encouragement given by everyone who was involved in the project.

Now, here, my last words for the reader of this book. Whether you know him or his work already or you are completely new to the author and know nothing about him or his work, open any page of the book freely and enjoy! We will be thrilled if you feel inspired and motivated enough reading this collection of his *Selected Poems* to further venture into the exploration of this lovable, inexhaustible poet Steve Dalachinsky and his wide-open world!

INTRODUCTION

INTRODUCTION

Michael Ruby

Steve Dalachinsky started writing poetry by the age of 11, but few people knew how good he was until his early 60s, and only then with a little help from a group of young poets in Brooklyn and admirers in France and Germany. Before that, he was better known as the short guy with a Brooklyn accent selling jazz records near SoHo art galleries by day and writing on scraps of paper in jazz clubs by night, a legend in the Downtown music scene. And before that, he barely survived his teens and twenties, a haze of abusive electroshock, psychiatric wards, and drug addiction in New York and Berkeley in the '60s and early '70s.

Dalachinsky was born on September 29, 1946, in the first year of the postwar baby boom. The grandson of Russian Jewish immigrants, the son of a house painter, he spent his first years in a two-family house on East 7th St. in Brooklyn's Midwood neighborhood, according to a series of interviews[1] before his death from a stroke on September 16, 2019. The family soon moved to a nicer house a few blocks away, but Dalachinsky was traumatically attacked by a mob of kids at the apartment building across the street for being "rich." His parents eventually couldn't afford the place, so they moved back to East 7th—a mixed area of Jews and Italians—for good. He first attended P.S. 217 and then P.S. 99, where Woody Allen had gone a decade earlier.

An arty and precocious kid, he was "drawing a lot, writing poetry and had my first true love" at the age of 10 or 11. In "the sorrows of young worthless,"[2] his amusing short memoir about living in Downtown New York, Dalachinsky writes of himself at 13 or 14: "Besides singing doowop on the corner in front of the pizza place, I wanted to play drums like Krupa, paint like Picasso or Dali, and write like myself (whoever that was)." He wrote short stories, too, and began collecting records, the beginning of his life as an audiophile. His mother, the dominant figure in his early years, intensely encouraged his artistic interests. But there was a dark side to her focus, the countless doctor's appointments to correct his feet and determine if he had allergies, when there wasn't anything wrong. Much later in life, he came to understand her malady as the search for the "perfect child." In the poem "giverny – trial & error # museum," he writes about "my mother who loved me so much it hurt / & me not knowing still if to love means to inflict pain." He said "things started

1. Unless otherwise indicated, quotes from Steve Dalachinsky come from interviews conducted by Michael Ruby in 2017–2019.

2. Steve Dalachinsky, "the sorrows of young worthless," www.greatweatherformedia.com /greatweatherformediacom/2019/9/16/steve-dalachinsky-the-sorrows-of-young-worthless. Accessed on November 19, 2025.

going awry" around "bar mitzvah time." After his dog Blackie fell down the stairs and broke its back, Dalachinsky began to have "temper tantrums." He would punch holes in many a window and door. He wasn't the perfect child.

His mother thought her imperfect son needed help, and his much-older brother's wife knew a psychiatrist on Flatbush Ave. So began Dalachinsky's unnecessary teenage odyssey through American psychiatry in the early 1960s, the very years when Ken Kesey was writing *One Flew Over the Cuckoo's Nest*. Early in the treatment, the doctor asked him to bring along his girlfriend, and "the doctor said / you were no good for / me," a traumatic experience Dalachinsky wrote about in "lament #2" in his best-known book, *The Final Nite and Other Poems*, one of several poems about living in "the thin hellish light." Then, Dalachinsky recalled, "he says to my parents, 'The best thing for Steven is shock treatments,' so he gives me all this shock treatment... on a table in a little room in his office." Dalachinsky said of his mother, "She was destroying me in an attempt to be whatever she thought was perfect. Corrective shoes and shock treatment, I guess for her, meant the same thing." Taken out of school during the treatments, he experienced the deepest alienation one afternoon sitting in his front yard in a daze reading Leon Uris's blockbuster *Exodus* (1958) while the neighborhood kids came home. "i felt only life's Exodus / watching bodies pass / on a warm fall day," he would later write in "the bones." He was plagued for the rest of his life by the thought that he suffered brain damage from the electroshock, according to his wife, Yuko Otomo.

Finally, the quack told his parents "I was very mentally ill and should be put away... All of a sudden, I find myself in Kings County Hospital on Ward 5," the juvenile psychiatric ward in Brooklyn's biggest public hospital. He instantly realized he "didn't belong there. I was the only one who wasn't in a street gang. Even the kids didn't know why I was there." Because he was small and different from everyone, a gang leader named Fats took him under his wing until Dalachinsky made a mistake in the dining room involving dibs on food, and then a group of kids beat him in the bathroom and stole from him at will afterward.

After "three months or so" at Kings County, his parents committed him to Hillside, a private hospital in Queens, where he spent around a year and a half in the early 1960s. Hillside was "the opposite of Kings County." A number of the teenagers "were the hippest people you'd ever wanna meet... For them, I was this young hip guy—and I wrote poetry, God!" A fellow inmate, Steve Fenchel, turned him on to John Coltrane and Ornette Coleman, the beginning of a lifetime of involvement with free jazz. Dalachinsky would hop the fence around Hillside to steal records from a Woolworth's store, one time returning with a Ray Charles album for himself and Charles Mingus for Fenchel. One of Fenchel's visitors, Allen Cohen, "was the first living poet I ever met" and became a lifelong friend.

One day, Dalachinsky had a life-changing experience. Another friend, Big Mike, "walks into my room and says, 'I got these two presents for you, man . . .' In one hand he's holding *A Coney Island of the Mind* (1958) and in the other he's holding *Howl* (1956). So I start reading these books. [The poem] 'Howl,' it was okay. But 'America, go fuck yourself with your atom bomb'?[3] Wow, you can say that? And Ferlinghetti's 'Christ climbed down / from His bare Tree'?[4] You can talk about Jesus that way?" He always looked back on Big Mike's gifts as "the biggest turning point" in his poetry, "when free verse completely hit me in the head." What he took away from the books was that he could write about anything he wanted. Before that, his poetry was always "romantic," which he derided as "moon in June," its diction influenced by his favorite poems in school, Blake's "Auguries of Innocence" and Herrick's "Gather ye rosebuds . . ." Around the same time at Hillside, "I discovered e.e. cummings, and he's the guy who influenced my writing in lowercase and all over the page." Later, he began to use the New York School's ubiquitous "&," and he was an early adopter of the Internet Age's "@."

To make his time at Hillside more fun, Dalachinsky asked his doctors for the drugs his friends were prescribed. Unable to admit there was nothing wrong with him, the doctors turned him down with vague words. With a little advice from Fenchel, Dalachinsky found a way around the doctors. At night, he started pestering the nurses that he couldn't sleep, he needed Nembutal to sleep. On the third try, they gave him "a couple of downs, and I followed Fenchel's advice, I stayed up all night. And boy, do you get stoned on downs!" This was the beginning of more than 10 years of heavy drug use, culminating in heroin addiction.

When the family's insurance ran out, the teenager returned home and was sent from Hillside to Midwood High School, where he felt "completely alienated." He was stigmatized both by other kids and by the authorities, which wasn't always a negative, such as when he reported to his draft board or applied for benefits. His first poetry notebooks date from this time, including several poems titled "my name is steven d. dalachinsky," written a month after his 16th birthday, and copies of poems written before he was committed. He won an art scholarship for high school students from Pratt Institute one year, but was channeled into the sculpture program when he really wanted to paint. After school and on weekends, he visited his girlfriend at Hillside, where they had clandestine sexual trysts, or hung out in Washington Square Park in Greenwich Village, where he met new friends and would "constantly steal books from bookstores." He tagged along after Harry Smith and Gregory Corso. The first live jazz he heard, through the back door of a Village club, was free jazz pianist Cecil Taylor. At the end of his senior year in 1964, he learned

3. Allen Ginsberg, *Howl and Other Poems* (San Francisco: City Lights Books, 1956), 39.
4. Lawrence Ferlinghetti, *A Coney Island of the Mind* (New York: New Directions, 1958), 69.

that he didn't have enough credits to graduate, likely because of his commitment. Mistakenly advised to take an easy business course in summer school, Dalachinsky ended up lacking sufficient English credits for admission to Brooklyn College. That was the beginning of a lifelong disappointment: He never earned a college degree.

The next few years were so chaotic that Dalachinsky had a hard time remembering the chronology. He worked a job separating pearls in Manhattan and lived in an apartment near Pratt, where he set up an easel and devoted himself to painting, eventually concluding, "I just was not a good visual artist." He moved to a building where his Village friend Chris Lang lived, near the Museum of Natural History on Manhattan's Upper West Side, then a Puerto Rican neighborhood. He shared an apartment with Midwood friend Lenny Zolla, and Hillside friend Big John lived downstairs. People called his room at the back of the apartment "Steve's cave." One night, a gang "who thought we were taking their neighborhood away from them" crashed a party at Big John's. Dalachinsky suffered a broken nose and was nearly blinded by a boxcutter blow to the face. His injuries scuttled a plan to quit his pearl-sorting job and join Cohen in Berkeley.

Dalachinsky moved home to recover from his injuries, only to discover that, during his absence, his mother had thrown away his early artworks and short stories. Partly as a result, he didn't write many stories after that. But his early notebooks show a surge in poetic activity. His interest in jazz "became so heavy" that he was one of the lucky few to hear Albert Ayler live, at the Lafayette Theatre in early 1966. Later that year, he wrote what would be his earliest known poem about jazz in response to a Taylor performance, using one of cummings' innovations with "harp(ie)s" in the second line, a technique of turning one word into two words that Dalachinsky often used. He attended Brooklyn College night school for a year, quitting "because my creative thinking was already coming out, and the school system was always asking me to remember other people's thoughts. I just couldn't balance it out." California dreamin' was his other reason for quitting, a decision he always regretted.

Dalachinsky and Zolla went to California in the summer of 1966, one year before "The Summer of Love," encamping in Berkeley, where Cohen had an apartment. Dalachinsky hung out on the university campus doing drugs and writing poetry, including his first haiku, but didn't think to connect with the poetic activity around the Bay. He fell in love with a runaway named Liz who sold the *Oracle* alternative newspaper in Haight-Ashbury. To Dalachinsky, the scene there "just looked so artificial to me. They didn't seem like reality. Little did I know they became the main reality." The young beatnik couldn't relate to hippies, even though he looked like them and took drugs, because they weren't into jazz. His summer soured when Liz got busted for shoplifting and was forced to return to her wealthy Chicago-area family.

Friends visiting from Brooklyn found him unknowingly poisoning himself on wood roses, a hallucinogen similar to morning glory. It was time to go home. After a second trip a year later and a "brush-off" from Liz, Dalachinsky's California dreamin' came to an end.

For a few years, Dalachinsky's life stabilized. He went into business with his cousin Bruce Cohen, opening a head shop in Brooklyn's Park Slope neighborhood. He lived nearby and had a long relationship with Monica Sheehan. Despite his distaste for hippies, he and Sheehan went to the Woodstock music festival in 1969, and he loved be-ins. He put one on himself in Prospect Park that attracted 300 people, he said, and described a Central Park be-in as "in my memory, fantastic." Eventually, the cousins had a falling out over the head shop, where Dalachinsky worked and Cohen was more of an investor. After that, his cousin "drew up papers and dissolved our partnership and gave the shop to me. I had a great accountant who was getting me out of paying taxes. Then, unfortunately, around that same time, the accountant got in a major car accident, and when he came back to help me, he was like a different guy, half-catatonic. And then I started shooting a lot of dope [heroin], and my girlfriend Monica left me. It was just a crazy time."

One day in the summer of 1970, Dalachinsky and a friend were listening to Eric Dolphy in his apartment. "I went into the tiny bedroom, stoned out of my mind. He fell out on the couch." The fan was going and a candle burning. "All of a sudden I woke up and I was surrounded by flames." Near the candle, he had two notebooks, both completely destroyed, a disaster for Dalachinsky. Based on his surviving notebooks, it appears that he lost everything between January 1968 and the summer of 1970. The only pieces he remembered and rewrote were the poem "woodstock" and the one-act play *the unbearable ubu*. He started a new poetry notebook a few months later, in December 1970, but wasn't as prolific for several years afterward.

After his poems burned and the head shop failed, Dalachinsky sank deep into heroin addiction. He moved back to his parents' house in Midwood. One day, his cousin brought a guy over who said, "I took a lot of drugs, too. I got a place you might want to go to." It was a halfway house called Journey Alert in Manhattan, now almost forgotten, one of a number of offshoots of Daytop Village, a drug-addiction treatment program. In "the sorrows of young worthless," summing up these chaotic years, Dalachinsky writes, "I spent most of my formative post-beat years between the West and East Villages, getting high, writing poems, hanging out in . . . strange people's apartments, listening to music, getting high, having sex, getting high, GETTING HIGH."[5] Dalachinsky's stay at Journey Alert would free him from heroin addiction for life, though not quite from drugs. Not yet.

---

5. Dalachinsky, "the sorrows of young worthless."

By the late '60s, his friend Lang had moved to 192 Spring Street in what was then known as the South Village, later as SoHo. In a few years, after Lang had become the building's superintendent, Dalachinsky snagged a vacant apartment and would live there for the rest of his life, not entirely happily. The apartment was the first door after the entrance, one of the skinniest one-bedrooms ever, a railroad flat with a sole window over Spring St., a bathtub in the kitchen, and a tiny bedroom in back. The toilet was outside in the hall. Dalachinsky's mother co-signed the lease and helped financially in other ways. He worked delivering vegetables to restaurants at daybreak and later in the office of a moving company. His drug use "went from banging to just eating downs again, a lot of bootleg Quaaludes." After a few months, he started having grand mal seizures on the Quaaludes and quit downs altogether. He still drank, in bars with his girlfriend Sherri Whitman between late 1973 and early 1975, writing many poems that were revised and published decades later, as well as the poem "anti-christ," with its refrain "not now."

Not much is known about Dalachinsky's life in the mid-to-late '70s. He worked odd jobs and visited the Bay Area again in late 1976. This time, he "kept away from a lot of activity and started reading more and more Kerouac . . . There was a period where I read at least four Kerouac novels in a row." He also read *Scattered Poems*, the *Trip Trap* haiku collaboration, and "*Mexico City Blues* a lot. I found a lot of solace in his poetry because of a certain freedom he had." Dalachinsky devoted much of his own poetic efforts toward writing haiku and connecting with the haiku subculture in American poetry. The terse form, which generally involves the juxtaposition of two different images, had a permanent effect on his writing, attuning him more to his natural surroundings and helping curb a tendency toward prolixity. No surprise, perhaps, that a Japanese poet and painter would now enter his life.

When Yuko Otomo met Dalachinsky in 1978 and moved in with him in 1979, he was totally clean, "a poster child for recovery from drug addiction," according to a series of interviews with Otomo in 2024 and 2025. He didn't even like her drinking wine. At the beginning of their 40 years together, Dalachinsky and Otomo led a quiet life imbued with art, listening to the often rare jazz albums he had collected, writing poetry and painting, going to museums, occasionally splurging on a jazz club. Neither Otomo nor Dalachinsky had a study or even a desk. He wrote on the couch in their tiny living room and out on the street, while she wrote and painted at the kitchen table. From the start, Dalachinsky encouraged Otomo to write in English, not Japanese, so she would reach more readers, eventually leading to her poetry books *Study*, *Anonymous Landscapes*, and *Pink*, among others. Shortly after they got together, Dalachinsky, at the age of 32, wrote one of his first mature poems, "spring," which, not unlike a haiku, intertwines two apparently unrelated phenomena: the arrival of spring and the death of an acquaintance. For the first time in years, he was filling notebooks at a rapid rate, including early ekphrastic poems in response to Monet and de Chirico in 1978 and 1979, the same year he met Beat poet and surrealist artist Ted Joans, who would soon help his poetry cross the Atlantic. This was the beginning of an outpouring of poetry that would last the rest of Dalachinsky's life.

The new couple often hung out on a concrete ledge at Spring Street and West Broadway, as their SoHo neighborhood became the arts capital of America. Janus Budde sold handmade jewelry there, Jean-Michel Basquiat sold postcards, and other artists stopped by. One day, Dalachinsky decided to try selling records. He had a pile of old records with a pop or skip, which the audiophile couldn't abide, including first pressings he later regretted selling. At first, he would just bring one or two records. He was surprised people wanted vinyl. Records were supposed to be on their way out. People were giving them away. As his records accumulated, he lugged them to the ledge first in a bag, then a shopping cart, then a dolly. Later, he sold cassette tapes, copied albums onto cassettes for people, and made mixtapes. Dalachinsky linked the beginning of his mature poetry to this "working on the street," where he felt a strong need to transform what he saw: "If I saw the car, it had to be more than a car. It had to fit into the landscape in a different way."

Dalachinsky's second artistic revelation came in April 1980, almost 20 years after his encounter with the Beats. He was writing a lot of "I feel sorry for myself poems," and his poet friend Patrick Keenan "told me, 'All your bones feel sorry for myself, a father kind of bones,' blah blah, the diarrhea of the mouth, and I got very offended, and a short time after that I wrote 'the bones' and said, 'Here, Patrick, read this one, this is another confessional, diarrhea poem.' And he read it and said, 'No, man, this is completely different, you've made some kind of breakthrough.'" Dalachinsky said he eventually realized he had learned how to transform his experience, not just describe it. No surprise his poetic breakthrough came in a poem about electroshock, which ends with the lines: "you gave me my bones / then you took them away."

In the early 1980s, he "started writing way more poems about visual art." Several poems for Arshile Gorky and "the extinction of useless lights" for Yves Tanguy, included here, "were written in a very transformative way, especially those two [museum] shows. I would start at the top of the Guggenheim and write something through rather than about—through, that's a very important word—every painting. Anything you're writing through and not about, even if you don't feel it, you're opening up the space." Dalachinsky was ekphrastic not in writing poems *about* paintings, but that *began* with paintings. And when he started writing his music poems, he didn't describe the performances. He wrote poems that began with the performances—or even before the performances—and went their own way.

A catalog of Dalachinsky's notebooks, compiled by Otomo, also reveals that while writing "the bones" and other poems in 1980, he was looking backward. He started a new notebook for the sole purpose of collecting and rewriting all of his haiku since 1966. From then on, he always had a notebook devoted to haiku. During a three-week visit to his old friend Zolla's house in Woodstock in August 1982, his work in haiku and other Japanese forms reached a height in *Salamander Gathering*, an unpublished chapbook excerpted here. In the epigraph, a haiku in itself, he writes: "after the storm / salamander(s) gathering / by the roadside," using Cummings' parentheses again to make words say two things at once.

On the street selling records, Dalachinsky met many people, including pianist Matthew Shipp and poet and antiquarian bookseller Harry Nudel. When the concrete ledge at the corner was carted away, a casualty of West Broadway's transformation into Art Gallery Row, Nudel invited Dalachinsky to share the overflow books table outside his store at 135 Spring St. Otomo paints a lively picture of the scene in her introduction to Shipp's *Black Mystery School Pianists and Other Writings*: "Their 'open air store' became one of the most intellectually charged 'salon/courts' in the neighborhood for many local artists, known and unknown equally, who dropped by to engage in conversations on various topics . . . Many artists, musicians, and writers such as Nam June Paik, Robert Wilson, Donald Judd, Tuli Kupferberg, Rashid Ali, Herman Cherry, Jonas Mekas, James Blood Ulmer, Vito Ricci, Peter Pinchbeck, Richard Kostelanetz . . . had their lofts nearby."[6] Throughout the '80s and '90s, Dalachinsky sold records, cassettes, and mixtapes there. He finally unloaded his unsold records around 2006, according to poet Jeffrey Joe Nelson, who helped Dalachinsky with them. "I used to joke with my friends: 'I might be poor and I might be sitting there on the street trying to sell a five-buck record, but hey, every time me and my wife go to Grand Union [supermarket], we can stop in 10 art galleries,'" Dalachinsky said.

Meanwhile, Ted Joans connected his friend with Bernhard Streit, a poet and publisher in Bern who helped arrange for a German translation of a Dalachinsky poem to appear in an anthology of contemporary American poetry in 1983.[7] Dalachinsky's first significant publication came at the age of 36 in Germany in translation! He wrote a longish poem dedicated to Streit, "incomplete directions," whose first lines, "to write eternity / on a piece of paper," clearly echo "To see a world in a grain of sand," the opening line of Blake's "Auguries." The possibility of meeting Streit led to Dalachinsky's first of many trips to Europe. He traveled with Nudel and his wife that summer, stopping in Amsterdam and Brussels, then for longer

6. Matthew Shipp, *Black Mystery School Pianists and Other Writings*, with an introduction by Yuko Otomo (Brooklyn: Autonomedia, 2025), 12.
7. *Sweet Little Sixteen* (Jugend in den USA), edited by Jurgen Schoneich (Hamburg: Rowohlt Taschenbuch Verlag, 1983).

in Paris, where Dalachinsky stayed at Shakespeare & Co. He immediately fell in love with Paris, where he could luxuriate in all of the artworks, writing more of his early ekphrastic poems, such as "Roualt (misery & war)," and where the city itself became an artwork for him to respond to in his poems. A Francophile who didn't know French, Dalachinsky enjoyed deliberately mangling the language in poems, just as he often did with English. He traveled to Europe again with Nudel in 1990, this time also with Otomo. Many poems and fragments from those two trips would appear decades later in *Where Night and Day Become One: The French Poems*, one of several books Dalachinsky was writing over many years without realizing it.

Other pieces of Dalachinsky's eventual public identity fell into place in the mid-1980s. When Lang moved away, Dalachinsky took over as super on Spring Street. In exchange for free rent, he was responsible for taking out the garbage, shoveling snow, and conveying complaints to the landlord of the roughly 20-unit tenement. He would immortalize the experience in his book *A Superintendent's Eyes*, mostly from the late '90s, but whose earliest poem was written in 1985. At the same time, Dalachinsky began to write in jazz clubs, including a poem for the Art Ensemble of Chicago in 1985, two poems for saxophonist David Murray in 1985–1986, and two poems for trumpeter Don Cherry in 1986, all published long afterward in *Reaching into the Unknown*. Also in 1986, he wrote "the mantis" for Taylor, which became the title poem of a book many years later. In "the mantis," Dalachinsky pulls off another of his seemingly unrelated pairings, the legendary pianist and the predatory insect.

Dalachinsky's frugal life of rarely seeing live performances changed with the 1987 opening of the Knitting Factory, an avant-garde venue that was more affordable than the established clubs. He and Otomo went almost nightly and soon became favorites of co-owner Michael Dorf, who comped them to every show. That was the beginning of Dalachinsky's life of listening to live jazz eight nights a week, becoming a fixture in the Downtown jazz scene. He was out much of the day, too, selling and talking to people on the street, going to museums or Anthology Film Archives, heaven for the lifelong cineaste. His appetite for art in many forms—and for artistic activity—became voracious. He attributed that partly to his increasing unhappiness with the "cave" of their apartment. Like a clogging artery, the railroad flat was forever narrowing as the floor-to-ceiling shelves sagged and overflowed with manuscripts, collages, records, books, and jazz ephemera. The space affected his poetics. He said he "deformed words because it gave some interest and fun to his cramped life."

When Dalachinsky first heard then-homeless tenor player Charles Gayle perform at the Knitting Factory on June 25, 1987, it was akin to a religious experience. From then on, Dalachinsky made recordings of, documented personnel for, and wrote poetry at every Gayle performance for two decades until 2006, when the poems were collected in *The Final Nite and Other Poems, Complete Notes from a*

Charles Gayle Notebook 1987–2006. In her introduction to the second edition in 2025, Otomo writes, "In Charles, we saw and witnessed the ability & possibility of extending the spiritual boundary of this particular music left behind by John Coltrane & Albert Ayler." Dalachinsky's "quest to write poems every time he saw Charles play, without failing,"[8] was an almost fanatical discipline, an esthetic of total immersion and comprehensiveness that brings to mind his master Kerouac's *Mexico City Blues* and works by Dalachinsky's contemporary, Clark Coolidge, whose very different jazz book, *The Rova Improvisations*, was finished a year earlier in 1986. The biggest difference between Dalachinsky's improvisations and those of Kerouac and Coolidge is that Dalachinsky's were written while listening to live music. They were what Shipp called "live-action writing of poems while attending jazz concerts."[9]

In Dalachinsky's own introduction, he says he included every poem written while listening to Gayle, "regardless of whether I thought them successful or not, & formatting aside, they are for the most part spontaneous with little or no editing after the fact."[10] The esthetic of completeness extends to unsuccessful poems, the idea that there's something valuable in our bad days, too. His qualification "formatting aside" points to the importance of spacing for Dalachinsky, some of which happened "after the fact,"[11] when he was typing the handwritten poems. He adds that the poems "oftentimes incorporate & relate, in an 'open field' manner, to the actual physical space where the music occurred." Expanding on that point, he said in the late interviews, "Someone told me Olson had this idea of open field writing, which was incorporating everything that's around you. That's what a lot of these poems did. And so the starting point may not always be the music."

Soon, Dalachinsky was trying to write at every show he attended, a goal for more than two decades. The poems are, by definition, improvisational. Few poets have written as many poems in response to live jazz performances, especially free jazz. Despite his history as an audiophile, Dalachinsky always privileged live music for his verbal improvisations. According to Otomo, he wrote on scraps of paper, then typed them up late at night at home. In his 2017 interview with the chronicler of the free jazz scene, bassist William Parker, Dalachinsky described his music poems as "collaborating with the guy on stage but they don't know it." His poem isn't about the performance, it's part of the performance, rarely describing the music or what the performers are doing.

---

8. Steve Dalachinsky, *The Final Nite & Other Poems: Complete Notes from a Charles Gayle Notebook 1987–2006* (Brooklyn: Ugly Duckling Presse, 2006, 2024), iii–iv.
9. Shipp, *Black Mystery School Pianists*, 7.
10. Dalachinsky, *The Final Nite*, vii.
11. William Parker, *Conversations III* (Paris: RogueArt, 2019), 485.

Only a year into *The Final Nite* poems, Dalachinsky wrote three poems at Cecil Taylor shows in 1988, and from then until 2008, he simultaneously wrote what would become his book *The Mantis*. It seems likely the unfolding Gayle book helped him view poems from Taylor performances as part of another book, which ended up being highly selective, not comprehensive like *The Final Nite*. All told, Dalachinsky wrote many hundreds of poems at jazz performances in the later '80s, '90s, and early 2000s. His style in these poems was probably closest to that of Amiri Baraka, whom Dalachinsky knew fairly well by the mid-'80s. During those years, Baraka increasingly was writing poems in response to jazz, culminating in *Wise, Why's, Y'z* in 1995. Like Dalachinsky's, Baraka's poems aren't always directly related to the jazz subject. They differ in not necessarily being tied to live performances.

In the mid-'90s, as he neared age 50, the relatively unpublished Dalachinsky made a little headway, with twin chapbooks ambitiously titled *People* and *Places*, each roughly 20 pages long, from New Jersey Beat poet Herschel Silverman's Beehive Press. In addition to writing in clubs constantly, Dalachinsky turned the camera on himself and his marginal economic status as a super and street vendor in the late '90s, writing the poems and prose of his first full-length published book, *A Superintendent's Eyes*. The first poem, "from the basement of the academy," with its address to "you fine poets who live among universities,"[12] establishes the point of view of a college dropout and American poetry world outsider. The book appeared in 2000, when Dalachinsky was 54, in a very small edition from Hozomeen Press, named after the mountain where Kerouac worked as a fire lookout. That same year, he pulled together *Subway Assemblages*, a 52-page chapbook written from 1987 to 2000, "mingling my thought and language with that of the many signs, advertisements, news print and lives found in subway cars," according to Dalachinsky's introduction for JVC Books. These two books marked the beginning of a flood of publications.

Other pieces of Dalachinsky's eventual identity that emerged in the '90s were the performer and emcee. At the Knitting Factory, Dorf offered Dalachinsky the chance to put on little shows in a back room—poetry, film, music—whatever he wanted. Now that he was a "curator," Dalachinsky would joke, he finally met many poets, musicians, and artists. In 1996, he became involved with founders of the Vision Festival, an annual highlight of far-out jazz in New York. He was an early emcee for Vision, reaching a larger audience with his street-corner gift of gab and "encyclopedic knowledge of jazz,"[13] in the words of Shipp, for whom Dalachinsky wrote the first of many liner notes. Dorf stepped up again when, in the late '90s, he offered to put out

12. Steve Dalachinsky, *A Superintendent's Eyes* (New London, Conn.: Hozomeen Press, 2000; Brooklyn: Unbearable Books/Autonomedia, 2013), 13.
13. Shipp, *Black Mystery School Pianists*, 7.

a CD of Dalachinsky's poems, but only if he performed them with musicians around the Knitting Factory, such as Parker and Shipp. His work on the CD, titled *incomplete directions* after the 1983 poem, was the beginning of years of performing with musicians. Before then, he hadn't performed and had only rarely read his poems in public.

Dalachinsky's biggest stage would be Europe, starting with an October 2000 tour of three German cities arranged by Norbert Nowotsch, a professor in Muenster who met Dalachinsky through Streit. That was the beginning of almost annual trips overseas for the rest of his life, years of writing poems and performing there. In the summer of 2001, the Israeli saxophonist Assif Tsahar, a New School student, offered Dalachinsky and Otomo his Paris apartment for a month. In Paris, the young French musical theorist Alexandre Pierrepont, who had sought out Dalachinsky in New York, brought him to the Left Bank stall of jazz photographer and bookseller Jacques Bisceglia, with whom Dalachinsky would later collaborate. Then, over dinner at his Paris apartment, Pierrepont introduced Dalachinsky to Michel Dorbon, founder of the RogueArt record label. In exchange for liner notes on RogueArt CDs, Dorbon and his wife would generously put up Dalachinsky and Otomo in their apartment whenever the couple wanted to visit France, allowing Dalachinsky's "Francophilia to flourish," according to Otomo. At a reading later in the visit, he met Franck Andrieux, who would translate Dalachinsky's poems into French after his death, as would Jürgen Schneider into German. During those years in Paris, Dalachinsky poured out the 40-page cycle of poems *Trial & Error in Paris* in 2001; the ekphrastic chapbook *St. Lucie*, a series of poems in 2003–2004 based on Zurburan's painting in Chartres Cathedral of the saint holding her eyes on a plate; and several long poems that later appeared in *Where Night and Day Become One*. Like other American poets from Edgar Allan Poe to Harry Matthews, Dalachinsky would be better known in France than in the U.S.

Closer to home, Dalachinsky was embraced by participants in the artistic renaissance in Brooklyn. *The Brooklyn Rail*, a monthly founded in 2000, soon made him its jazz columnist. His "Outtakes" column was awaited by jazz fans every month for almost two decades. This *Rail* perch set up the frugal poet to be comped at most jazz clubs in New York, including places he could never afford. He could finally attend as many shows as he wanted—and he did, often towing along young friends as his "comp +1." Also in the early 2000s, he met Marisol Limon Martinez, Ryan Haley, James Hoff, Julien Poirier, and others connected with Brooklyn's Ugly Duckling Presse at their "anti-reading" in the basement of the venue Tonic. At home afterward, Dalachinsky said, "Yuko, now we've found our kids!" Characteristically self-deprecating, he added, "They're so intelligent, much smarter than me and you."

In truth, Dalachinsky was displaying his intelligence daily. In addition to his outpouring in jazz clubs and France, he took on several large ekphrastic and collaborative projects. He wrote the delicate "portuguese letters" in 2000, based on phrases in the 17th-century *Letters of a Portuguese Nun* that influenced Rilke. In 2002, he began his largest ekphrastic work, the collaboration *Flying Home* with German painter Sig Bang Schmidt, whom Dalachinsky met in New York in the '90s. The combination of paintings and 50-plus deceptively simple poems about World War I, published a decade later in France, is an imaginative inhabiting of the supposed "war to end all wars." While working with Schmidt, he undertook another ekphrastic work, the chapbook *Midnight/Noon – the insomnia poems*, 17 poems based on 220 "Insomnia Drawings" by Louise Bourgeois. Combined with his ekphrastic writing in France in 2003–2004, these sequences reach a level of extended engagement with visual art that approaches his work with Gayle and Taylor. His most extensive collaboration, with experimental poet Jim Leftwich, also began in 2004, with a series of short, often neological sound poems descended from Dada. The two collaborated via email for the rest of Dalachinsky's life.

This intense period of ekphrastic writing corresponds with the renewal of Dalachinsky's youthful interest in being a visual artist. He started making collages "on and off in the '80s," and then in his last 15 years made "thousands and thousands," usually at the cramped kitchen table. In the middle of a phone call or an interview, Dalachinsky might be cutting images out of consumer magazines or invitations to art openings, two favorite sources. He said his participation in the mail art movement made him "more and more involved [with collage]. It gave me the reason to do something." The first of several chapbooks of collages, *Fake Hits of the '60s*, was published in 2005.

In the early 2000s, Dalachinsky was constantly publishing chapbooks with small presses, including his and Otomo's kitchen-table operation, Sisyphus Press. At least seven chapbooks were published in 2005 alone, an otherwise unhappy year in which he was diagnosed with prostate cancer. But he transformed his radiation treatments into the full-length poetry book *The Invisible Ray*, partly written in the south of France, where he was invited to a music festival and then toured on the road with percussionist Didier Lasserre and sax player Sébastien Capazza. The book, published a decade later by Overpass Books, takes an open field approach to the experience, much like his contemporaneous writing in jazz clubs. A couple of the chapbooks were published by "the kids @ Ugly Duckling" and the Loudmouth Collective, which included several UDP people. The relationship culminated in UDP's 2006 publication of *The Final Nite*, Dalachinsky's first trade publication with a significant print run. The book, recently reprinted and briefly excerpted here, won the PEN Oakland/Josephine Miles prize, bringing Dalachinsky's name to a broader American poetic audience for the first time at the age of 60, though he continued to be far better known in the free jazz world than in the poetry world, even among New York School and Language poets with whom he shared poetic lineages.

That same year in Paris, Bisceglia suggested they collaborate on a book of photos of jazz greats and poems in response to their performances. The offer was a stroke of luck that gave Dalachinsky the chance to bring together poems written at jazz clubs for decades. He unearthed some early gems, including one from the '60s about spotting Mingus with a camera in Tompkins Square Park, and Mingus saying, "Shhh. I'm not Charles Mingus today. I'm a photographer."[14] The 429-page book, *Reaching into the Unknown, 1964–2009*, which should be much better known in the U.S., was published by RogueArt in 2009. It appeared a year after Dalachinsky's other book with the press, *Logos and Language: A Post-Jazz Metaphorical Dialogue*, a hybrid collaboration that included a lengthy interview of Shipp from the early 2000s, 17 poems in response to Shipp performances from the 1980s until 2007, and Shipp's own writings.

Dalachinsky rounded out this immense gathering of four decades of jazz poems with his first love, Taylor, writing the last poems for the 53-page chapbook *The Mantis* (2008), published by Iniquity Press. And finally, in a burst in October 2009, listening to British sax player Evan Parker, Dalachinsky wrote most of the poems in his last jazz book, the chapbook *Long Play*, published in France in 2011. With the publication of this immense oeuvre in response to free jazz, Dalachinsky was known for the rest of his life as "a jazz poet," which bothered him because he felt it obscured his other writing. While his devotion to live jazz remained fanatical, he only wrote poetry occasionally in clubs thereafter.

Like other poets of his generation, Dalachinsky drew from the poetic innovations since Whitman and Rimbaud. He started out as a second-generation Beat after reading Ginsberg and Ferlinghetti, reveling in their permission to say whatever he wanted, and always maintained ties with Beats. He was close friends with Joans, visited the dying Corso several times in 2000–2001, and devoured Kerouac's poetry books, which came out long after their author's death. Through the Beats, as well as the early abuse he suffered and his lifelong poverty, he developed a highly critical view of American society and history. Various Modernist approaches also filtered down to him: the Orphism of Apollinaire and Cendrars; the short line of Ginsberg's mentor, William Carlos Williams. Directly from Cummings, he picked up his lack of capitalization and punctuation, his minimalist spacing, and also his decomposition of words, which later led Dalachinsky into Dadaism. Like some other Beats, he was drawn to Japanese poetry, though not for its Buddhism, but for its precise

14. Steve Dalachinsky, *Reaching into the Unknown 1964–2009*, with Jacques Bisceglia (Paris: RogueArt, 2009), 238.

and suggestive natural descriptions. He diverged crucially from the Beats, and from much of the New York School, in eschewing a direct approach to his nominal subject.

Dalachinsky often talked about poetry as "descriptive transformation." "The whole idea of transformative writing," he said, "is we disconnect from the thing in front of us without disconnecting from it. And what I mean is by always including that reality with the metaphysical reality." The initial transformation is seeing a thing as more than itself, which it always is. He often transformed a subject by putting it in relation to another subject, intertwining them in the poem. Later on, he applied his understanding of Black Mountain School founder Olson's projective verse to the moment of composition. Language Poetry, which flourished in New York in the '80s and '90s, as well as Dalachinsky's Dadaist leanings, gave him permission to be nonrepresentational. At the same time, his love affair with France pulled him back toward the representational Orphism of Apollinaire and Cendrars.

During his last decade, despite bouts of illness, Dalachinsky remained as close to ubiquitous as anyone in New York's Downtown music, art, and poetry scenes. Not so long before, he had been emceeing a set at the Vision Festival, then pushing his books and CDs at the RogueArt merch table during breaks, often with a quip in his Brooklyn accent, known to all. He devoted more energy to recording than ever before. Lasserre connected him with J.J. Arnould of Bam Balam Records in Bordeaux, who presciently paired Dalachinsky with the French art rock group The Snobs. They recorded three CDs: *Massive Liquidity* (2011), *ec(H)o-system* (2015), and *Pretty in the Morning* (2019). Dalachinsky also teamed up with his childhood friend, sax player Dave Liebman, on a CD of mostly early poems, *The Fallout of Dreams* (2014), for RogueArt.

Dalachinsky's obsession with collage spilled into his writing in the unpublished book *As Collage*, a series of 73 poems written in 2013–2015, where he treated each poem as a collage, according to Otomo. His prose-poetry chapbook *Black Magic* began as a cut-up of an English translation of the 1920s French novel *Magie Noir* by Paul Morand. He responded to America's growing inequality and worship of Mammon in the chapbook *Fool's Gold*, a series of 19 poems, and to the country's evident decline after the 2016 election in "the death of America," with its varying medial caesura and prophetic whisper:

> there's something happening here America is dying
> america can never be what we were told it could be
> but listen carefully it can be worse a lot worse

He continued his ekphrastic and collaborative work, this time with Otomo, in *Frozen Heatwave*, based on art exhibits they saw in 2017, which was published by Luna Bisonte. His collaboration with Leftwich was voluminous in 2018, including the posthumously published *be/ond seh flinges*, also from Luna Bisonte. Dalachinsky's Francophilia reached monumental form in *Where Night and Day Become One: The French Poems 1983–2017*, published by Great Weather for Media. The last of his large-scale works, along with *The Final Nite* and *Reaching into the Unknown*, the book collected decades of poems, dating back to his first visit in 1983. Dalachinsky's last poem—written in a club, of course—was "Lace," in response to a performance by harpist Zeena Parkins.

Several days before his death, preparing for an event on Long Island honoring Ray Johnson, Dalachinsky revised a 1995 poem dedicated to the mail-art pioneer, "we live with rats but don't know it." On the day of the event, Dalachinsky characteristically wedged in a matinee performance by the Sun Ra Arkestra before heading out of the city. When he collapsed shortly after reading the poem, his last words to Otomo were, "I'm sorry, I guess I OD'd on Sun Ra." Now, finally, everyone can begin to OD on Dalachinsky.

I. EARLIER POEMS

my name is steven d. dalachinsky

1.

it has come
i sense its presence
i hear it
i smell it
i feel it
but i cannot see it . . .

2.

creeping ever softly into the night —
shades of torment and delight . . .
bobbing around in strange lovely patterns —
to see it with the eyes — to feel it with the heart . . .
rich is the presence of the moonlight —
the presence of the ever-so-calm night . . .

monotony has set in . . .
that never-ending wearisome sameness . . .
. . . the beautiful soft comforting night —
man's most precious possession —

to see it — to feel it . . .

i do not see — i do not sense its presence . . .
i do not feel — i do not use this wonderful gift to man . . .
monotony has set in — i am weary — i must rest . . .

3.

to see with the eyes yet not to feel with the heart
is like seeing nothing at all . . . i do not see —
i do not feel — i am blind to the awareness of life . . .

4.

what is existence — a breath of air —
                    a piece of bread
                    a cigarette
                    a comforting bed —
i am unaware of existence . . .

5.

existence — the ever present feeling that death is staring
you
right
in
the
face . . . .

thank you for the street corner kiss

thank you for the street corner kiss
the piggy back ride
& i the same
the orange skies of black coffee
thank you for the open fly
in the hallway
your dripping thoughts
the trips to the neighborhood bars
the fake moans
& tight desires
thank you for not letting me in
but letting me stare impotently thru the doorway
the street corner kiss
the smear of sarcasm across your lips
my rigid trembling hands
& frigid heart   throbbing in my throat
thank you for the street corner kiss
the kick in the ribs
the shiv in the guts
the pointing finger that goes bang bang
you're DEAD

thank you for him
for leaving me for him
your full face
the scar
the burning corner kiss
the fucking burning street corner kiss
the innocence of knowledge
the coolness of childhood
the cold   you wiped across my eyes
my soft tongue caressing your thighs
the anger
imprisoned
rushing to meet you

in the emptiness
of blue
the fear   the fire   the flowers   your bosom   my come
thank you for your stinging songs   the naked moon
the pagan warmth   the calculated jabs   the prism turned pale
the street corner kiss   the street corner kiss
thank you for this   the street corner kiss

– 7/67 & 10/09/00

the unbearable ubu

(a play in one indefinite act)

DURATION: INDETERMINATE. CAN LAST FOR SECONDS. MOMENTS. HRS. DAYS. ETC.

SETTING: ANY FLAT SURFACE. PREFERABLY W/or/WITHOUT A PIECE OF 3X3 FT. FRESH OR ARTIFICIAL RICH GREEN ASTRO-TURF

PROPS: 1 12 OR 15 FT. LADDER (OR THE TALLER THE BETTER IN SOME CASES) WOOD or ALUMINUM. NO. WOOD. ONLY WOOD. WORN FADED OLD BROWN WOOD.

CHARACTERS or *CAST* AS THEY LIKE TO SAY: 2 MALES —*plus* & *minus.*

COSTUMES: *plus* WEARS A PLUSH LEOPARD SKIN (VERY FURRY) ROBE WITH A BRIGHT WHITE FURRY ERMINE COLLAR ATTACHED AT THE NECK BY A GOLD PENDANT. HE ALSO WEARS A TYPICAL ELABORATE KING'S CROWN & HOLDS A GOLDEN SCEPTER WITH A LION'S HEAD AT ITS TOP END. HE HAS ON A PAIR OF PURPLE VELVET & GOLD SLIPPERS THAT CURL UP DRAMATCALLY AT THE TOES. HE SPORTS A LARGE ERECTION. (& A BIT OF A PAUNCH.)

minus WEARS NOTHING BUT A FORESKIN. (essentially both men are naked.)

LIGHTS COME UP SLOWLY LIKE A SUNRISE. *minus* IS KNEELING ON ONE KNEE LOOKING UP TOWARD THE TOP OF THE LADDER WHERE *plus* RESIDES. HIS PENIS, THOUGH IT CAN NOT REALLY BE SEEN, IS SMALL AND LIMP.

minus: MASTER
minus: MASTER

(this goes on for a while)

minus: MAHHSTER (a bit hesitant — slowly rising)
plus too slowly rises

minus: MASTER (putting a foot on the first rung of the ladder)
minus continues to chant MASTER while slowly climbing the ladder rung by rung.
plus is now climbing down the ladder & suddenly begins to chant what sounds like MAH or STER but never the whole word. suddenly but almost imperceptibly *minus* does likewise.

exactly ½ way up or down the ladder depending on one's point of view, the robe, shoes, crown & scepter exchange hands & we can clearly see that *plus'* erection has diminished

while *minus'* has grown considerably. as they pass each other *minus* falls silent, now wearing the regalia & *plus* can be heard chanting MASTER MASTER over & over again. as *plus* reaches the bottom & *minus* the top, they each assume the position the other had had at the beginning of the play.

THE LIGHTS SLOWLY FADE LIKE SUNSET UNTIL THE STAGE IS COMPLETELY DARK. FIN.

— 4/02 rewrite of a play written in 1969 & lost in a fire that same year

anti-christ

I.

no christ
not now
maybe some flowers
a leaf
a wind
or a rush-hour news stand crowd
but no   christ
not any christ
don't ask why
not now
why is too obvious
someone always asks why
just accept that i can't accept it now
no icons
no gods
just their colors
fancy colors
fine legs
firm behinds
erect nipples in plush purple leotards
some warmth
cozy jagged piece of mind
but no christ not yet.

no gods

II.

just idols   golden in resplendent money shrines
and maybe some flowers
maybe later
and a leaf

but not now
a wind
but no prayer
a rush of people
a sun
a worm / the night
a candle and a cat
a hope
but no cross
not now
no star
heaven   maybe later
but galaxies   and milky ways
and a three musketeers
maybe a shower
some food
and a bed
but no virgin
not now
a leaf
nothing immaculate
a song
no christ
not here
a walk
maybe some place soon
some time
no blessings
some tears
maybe later
a wind . . .

whittling my legs
crossed
picking at my nails
licking my wounds
watching t.v.
i hang on

a wake
no action
maybe later
resurrection
erect
a song
a leaf
no tears
a poem
no plea
a hum
(some tears   oh please   some tears)
no christ
not now
a wind
no sermon
a door
no sacrifice
a pleasure
oh god   a pleasure
not now   please
a room
maybe later
a street
soon   soon   before i pass
a rush of people
but not now
    a window . . .

bar poems

from a poem i was writing in a dream

"...... the hot red embers of whispering wood."

bar (the dog)

3 legs
& a table
where Shakti
sat

the dog limped
in agony behind the bearded
dancer
drained

Shakti embraced Shiva
in a silent sway of circular pleasure
acting cool
as her yellow karma
spilt thru her pink-red kimono
like the stink of heavily perfumed
incest

finger cymbals tinkled .... joylessly

the dog limped behind
in drained agony.....

— 9/3/73

bar (the thief)

the thief who stole the worker's dollar
sat dreaming of nothing
writing nothing
to his goddess
that someone said was sweet

she did not even notice.

— 9/3/73

bar

the janitor
vacuumed dust
from the floors of the insane
the time was not right
but right as it was was
right there
gods looked @ my selfishness
she looked as usual far away
time came right come quick came looked
we looked she looked still looks
we fight we love we don't accept we're here
we're here we're where not here we're where?
we're here.

— 11/73

spring

for Robert

the Spring seems so familiar
a clean and ageless face that shows up every year
between here and the supermarket
while later at the checkout counter with eyes half open
i snap my memory's fingers   and try to place that face
though the name   Spring's name i just cannot recall

the tree that never stood is always there and will one day
without my knowledge or consent   bear leaves again
the grass is just a little greener
the chill a little warmer
the blue a little bluer
the greys less grey

this air of familiarity   reminds me of Robert
whose name i know   whose face either
clean shaven or bearded
easily appears behind my eyes
Robert
my age   homosexual   actor nice very nice guy
heavy drug user just reapplied for college
intelligent   lucid Robert   heart trouble
died around the same time Spring put in another appearance

embolism i was told   similar to something   my memory seems to under go

i would have written a separate poem for him
but why take the time
i only knew him briefly
his death was like adding another day to the calendar
without really affecting very much
his death was not like Spring's will be
for he will not come back again next year

Spring is not a homosexual
Spring tempts me to be happy
and to fall apart with love
but one can not wake up
if one has not yet slept
some times i avoided Robert on the street
i try to avoid Spring in much the same way

Spring is like Robert
   it affects me
                    yet it does not
  it is something interposed into the days
   and carried sweetly with the sunset
into night

Spring is like an embolism
   it doesn't belong here
                              yet it fits

i've had a bad year
i've criticized
i've lied
i've told the truth
i've cheated and been caught
i haven't slept
i'm tired
i've survived
                not meaning to
                not trying to
                not wanting to
i've come 'round again
     like Spring
and one day i'll be gone
                          like Robert

but enough of my troubles

the last time i saw Robert
he hobbled by on a crutch broken leg in tow
moving slowly
toward the liquor store
he smiled said hello
out of sheer habit i did the same
and he was gone
he asked nothing of me —

the other day near the supermarket
like a quick wind
on a tense face
bicycling thru red lights
Spring smiled at me
just for the sake of smiling
it too asked nothing
i smiled back out of sheer habit
not knowing exactly who or what Spring was
but realizing that i was taken in
for a moment
by its charm

the grass becomes a little greener
the sky more fresh
the chill is somewhat warmer
the greys less grey
the tree that never stood
is always there
and one day
leaves

so for now i'll call Spring Robert.

woodstock

for Monica

i saw you
naked
showering in the rain
in front of the trailer
the hippie tried to push some propaganda on us
but we preferred a bar of ivory soap.

dripping from the sky
we slosh thru the mud
down to the lake
and wade bare ass
through lilies
and weeds.

— 1979

De Chirico Landscapes

escaping hours
shattered against infinite waiting
of dumb sentiment.

i am a stuffed doll
staring thru your archway
at the shadow of your hairline
and the dead curve of your waistline
against the grey-brown ivy platform.

        flat form
                dying against the street
    hugging the ground
                        a steam cloud in space
heaving with a gourmet's glance
. . . . waiting to depart.

— 1979

Ted Joans

Ted Joans
has 10 Picassos
in Timbuktu
he says
the sand dunes in
the Sahara
are sensual and
soft
and refers to that desert
as
she

he carries secrets in a water sack
and his passport around his neck

he travels around the world
the way most folks travel around
the block

he knows everyone
everywhere

he has 2 hats in Spain
waiting to be broken
in
and an overcrowded pad
in Paree
(pardon my French)

his entire collection
of jazz records
has fallen into the
Niger River

the other night
he brought me a piece
of
sweet potato
pie.

the bones

you played with my bones
now my bones lie soft and frustrated
on your platter
picked by warmth
and stunned by complete repulsion

now the sanity of my situation
screams
like headaches
through the yellowing of what once looked like torso
and the skull
so hard to penetrate
is the only door
between plucking and righteousness.

you shocked my system
with more volts than my system could take
and as you helped me crawl from the slab
to the car
i thought only of the soft side of life
and as you sat me in my neutral state
in the chair in front of the house
i felt only life's Exodus
watching bodies pass
on a warm fall day.

the bones
the bones
connecting what was once
sometimes pleasant place to be

the soft and broken bones

you stuffed me in the back seat
and answered my birth right
with medicines

and the lack of medicines
you told me not to pick my nose
not to masturbate
but to remove my bones to some healthy place
failing to tell me that the sun
only shined
when you let it shine
and that alone in a room
with my bones   and
theirs
            sanity could only be found
under the pillow
                        or in the shower.

with the grinning breath
you occupied my bones
yet never managed to inhabit them

you rocked my bones
the bones
the bones
so shocked and softened
by neurotic industrial wastes

the novel bones
the sonnet bones
the philosophical bones of Dogs

with the structure further dissected
the frame became more insulated
insulted by its foundation
angered by the careless reconstruction
frightened by the entrance
into its own sweet core
the frame became unstable and rebellious
and the bones late cramped and stunned
howling in the revulsion
at their place in the world

and the bones
the bones
digested what was left of themselves
and rejected everything else
experimenting with poisons
and feeling the causes of this stricken State

now the bones yearn them to break through the flesh
and snap into place
on the hard cold air

now the bones feel nothing
but their own uncomfortable shifting about
in the tomb which you have built for them

and the bones know nothing of the freedom
you later sanctioned
for
the bones
the bones
have neither the chance to speak
the strength to moan
nor the desire to run

the bones don't cry they're too grown-up
the bones won't dance they're too shy
the bones don't want to move no too weak
the bones won't even love they're too stubborn

the bones can't shoot jagged through the tips
of my toes
they're too angry
yet always swollen with tears
the bones cannot refuse song
they are too humble

the bones are no longer mine
but the bones out there

i alter these bones
and willing or not
these bones do change
but the hard bone of skull remains
and these sounds that rip my ears
these sights that burn my eyes
carve like fine ivory
                    dead light
                      upon a pattern of memories
                          that connects
                              faces with feelings
and the faces turn to bone
and the bone turns to pale translucent ash
yet never disappears

you gave me my bones
then you took them away.

— December 1980

the first cemetery of spanish & portuguese synogogue (1656–1833)

inside chinatown's thigh
near the edge of st. james'
cross
by oliver street
& described as "OUTSIDE the CITY"
lies a dark acre of nameless tombstones
a sweet & sacrilegious monument
to judaism
consecrated in 1656
cornered by brick
& bridged by steel & clay
the ashes of ashes
the dust of dust
on this cold & dismal ash wednesday.

a triangle of empty benches
the prickly wild berry trees
lining the black wrought iron
speartipped gate

some secret inside the tombs
the vacant geometric forms
so worn & final
resting "en un espacio pequeño y solemne
para Shearith Israel"

a remnant of
a prayer for the souls
of the wandering dead
who now repose
in god's new world

— 3/4/81

Artaud le momo

mother earth mother there is always one that cannot be saved mother earth
dying mother earth dead mother momo suckling her young

CIGURI CIGURI — the true man before god destroyed him

ciguri oh foolish fool of fools treated with such shocking disgrace
poet poet poet
electrically shocked & twisted rearranged for the satisfaction of others

dead mama momo antonin on toes i lean on toes artaud
i shout & cry & scream tip toe momo
skin wrapped tight in desperation
god father christ yourself the mother sister phallus actor whore
puta puta peyote faced puta opiated puta momo mom
bad boy rugged handsome prominence
ciguri momo excreted skin
syrupy muscle soul
separately fused one atop the other
crawling with too much life
& the alien stickiness of it.

a system of justice tragic figure bent stooping upright
aged so old before your time
fingers mingling your mind reflected in glassbook descriptions
desert on the end table seeds of *Ciguri* stirring in your stomach
circling forever the soul the man the mother the momo the fingers
the nails driven home

monologue

for yuko

i am like a bad joke
the way i pound the pavement with your heart
looking for a hungry dream

i am a sinister plot
devised to make you feel uncomfortable
at restaurants

you have everything i want
except a few things
i have nothing i want

you need very little to get by on
i have very little
but it never seems enough

you accept me as i am
and are content just to be near me
i don't even know what i am is

you like to smoke coolness
and watch the flowers grow
i like to spoil your good time

you are a well that is easily filled
and sits smiling in the garden
and i can't see well enough alone.

from *Salamander Gathering*

(woodstock journal aug 7–aug 27, 1982)

after the storm
salamander(s) gathering
by the roadside

I am this grey sky

carried,
    snailing,
      thru poetry
like the beast that I am
   I wake
      overcast,
         in a bright room
with a line on my lips
  neither city nor country
but a part of the internal
  eternity that is me

the sky
   also overcast
      offers no consolation
   my eyes itch
     my nose runs
        my disposition sags
  like feet stuck in molasses
and I flop forward
  like an overly stuffed
          empty pillow at the waist

a cricket
   slowly crawls across the
      kitchen   counter
         a mammoth mosquito

positions itself motionless
on the windowsill

the goats are still asleep somewhere
down the road
I move my stool toward the
window as the LIGHT
tries to penetrate
and the firewood dries
there are spiders and webs in
every corner
moths flies and beetles
on every pane
the cat waits to be fed
the wet and leaning grass
seems to understand my
burden

we retreat from (the) LIGHT
and return to it again
we deny or forget the LIGHT
but it returns to us again
the LIGHT recedes from the logs
and the day is overcast again
she snaps pictures of
unfamiliar scenes
they settle on a stump
in front of a field of
white flowers
and smiles as the
LIGHT reappears and shines
from the barrette in her hair
the old chair is dying
as she opens the door
to tell me of the beautiful
blue dragonflies
near the pond

the coffee-stained out-of-
tune piano
is yellowed by disuse
but tonight
she will play me
a tune
that she recalls from her
childhood

(but now)
I will rise from this
station somehow
and move across
the floor
and out the door

I will carry the beast
a rise
like a fine mist
over water
and the butterfly
need never
understand.

8/10

heavy grey blue clouds
cover the (bright) sky
and the greens darken
like an approaching storm
the tadpole glides beneath the
pond's surface testing its new legs
and that one loud
insomniac cricket continues
all afternoon

(am i confused?)

out here the honey bees keep
 working and the flies keep
fucking around

(with me)

the cat returns from
 god knows where
after being gone all morning
 and now rests in my lap
 the hungry wasp finally
 remembers where the flowers are —

the useless awesome wasp
it is lunch for some
 dinner for others or rest

(for me a rare lunch)

the hummer has been all day
 along with the saw
 their echoes are thick
 the cat leaves

Overlook Mt. Trail

overlook mt. trail

silent

except for the foot steps
except for the buzzing
except for the pen scral

silent

except for the hammering
except for the thinking
except for the 3 empty beer cans

silent

except for our breathing
except for the sunlight touching the feet

silent

except for the red clay
except for the plucked flower

silent

the rustling

overlook mt. trail

silent

except for the stones
stray birds
& the passing 2 strangers

overlook mt. trail

is   silent
upward
directionless

except for the spider beneath
her sandal & the sound of her fingers
scratching

except for the path we follow
except for the rumors of summit
& the ghosts that in the abandoned hollow hotel
except for the patches of clear sky

silent

except for our fast fading shows

silent

except for our mounting excitement

silent

except for this all over silence

silent

yo soy un home del azul

I am a man of blue
   roasting in a meadow
      surrounded by pines

from across the meadow
   at a great distance

a flute that is only just beginning to sing
      reaches my ears

I am a man of blue

the crickets gladly dance
      on my backbone

this ribcage of clouds
dissolves into blueness
this day

the blue berry bushes burst
kneeling into the meadow

I am a man of blue

my fast drying sweat
the only testament to a meadow

from across the meadow
at a great distance

mountains that have long survived
only just now reach my eyes

the wind is water-falling through trees
the hawk has not returned

I am a man of blue
she is my mother

Rouault (misery & war)

for the walk &
for the stage
i exercise my passion
bulk rate
cubed & cut up
in the hot bellied street

there is the black & white misery of war
the startling color of electric illumination

there is the falling apart
in the growth

for the clown &
for the carpenter
i exorcise my passion
like a finely embroidered chair
floating quietly thru the
city of light.

—paris, 7/30/1983

incomplete directions

for Bernhard Streit

to write eternity
on a piece of paper
is so easy
then everything else follows:

walls
shadows
dreams
death
life
gurus
signs that say keep off the grass
signs that say don't feed the birds
signs that say not too fast
signs that say not too slow
this new generation of ours
already grown old
this new year
nothing

when i asked the man for directions
on how to get to eternity
he said just keep walking
& then you'll come to the end of the street
& when you get to the end of the street
just keep walking & you'll come to the end of the street
& when you get to the end of the street
just keep walking & you'll get to the end of the street
& when you get to the end of the street just keep walking
you get the idea

to write eternity on a piece of paper
is so easy
then everything else follows:

poets
drunkards
lovers
flowers
paranoids
ceilings
bombs
toilets
answers
fingers pointing
picking noses

to find eternity is very hard
to be eternity is very hard
signs that say
stop you are now approaching eternity
signs that say eternity is just around the corner
signs that say school crossing
signs that say at the end of this street eternity
slow down no alcoholic beverages no unnecessary noise
don't feed the pigeons don't squeeze the squirrels
at the end of this street eternity
then just keep on walking until you get to the end of this
street & when you get to the end of this street just keep on
walking
circles
doormats
windows
mirrors you spoke to yourself in your mirror
you decided to change by changing the
course of the street

that's o.k.
the course we've walked
is dead
but we keep walking
the new course will be similar
to the old

in just one way
when we get to the end of the street
we will just keep walking

but maybe we'll stop
stop searching
stop walking
sit down & rest
& kiss & talk & hug & fight & love & die
& never mention eternity
when we get to the end of the street
we'll stop
maybe even turn around if it's not too late
that's nice

it's nice to look for something that's hard to find
but such bullshit to write it down
nothing pretty or romantic about this poem
nothing at all to read
these signs that say more signs
danger
slippery
falling rock zone
deer crossing
sharp turn
heaven
hell

so easy to write heaven on a piece of stone . . . .
coda:
the old tall thin grey man
in the old tall thin grey suit
came toward me arms out beckoning
holding in his left hand
a small grey card
& saying in a thin sharp grey voice
i don't wanna die yet
i don't wanna die yet

i don't die yet
i turned & ran in panic to the white living room
slammed his fingers in the door
slammed the covers over my head

easy to write death
& then eternity follows
as easy to run away
or walk to the end of the street
& just keep walking

maybe if we reach the river
we can take the stone
& drop it in.

the extinction of useless lights

(Yves Tanguy retrospective)

your pale hands touch the moon
sighing always sighing
with an almost constant constancy
fingered lines etch across wastelands
hairlines like fine grass & straight geometry
sharp fingernail etchings
in dark & wounded gardens
accenting/extending sparse energies
filaments of other creatures
from dark seas or "other" planets
extinct or not yet seen
brain matter
wiggling across the different stations of day
sunset / sundown — *always afraid of night*
always bordering on NIGHT
like *AUTO* graveyards & grave grey sighs
tired desperate naïve & mad
(a skeleton of dark smoke rising up to startle us)
shy cluttered forms that hug the choking ground
from freedom to crowdedness
your alien insides wander with always the sky in sight
the SKY — a final HOPE
neither legend nor figure can trap the melodies of your bloated notes
from sweet space & alienation your form becomes bones
smooth polished stones that soften with each consecutive night
& your motion becomes concentrated until your movement ceases

in the heart of the tower
a prophet rubs his chin
& clouds of ghosts enter the world
soft kidney-creatures smile thru their wounds
& the clouds become THIS LIFE
from spaciousness to clutter
their alien insides wander
their shadows become a soft white tower

the more we are
the more we become our shadows
& our shadows then follow us about
the more we become
the more our sad forms recede
the less we are
the more ghostly our shadows appear
fade
disintegrate
into wind / dust / sky/ >
this is our possible salvation / wind moving sky
wind that is SKY flat sharp spaces of white

in the heart of the tower
there is a prophet
his shadow becomes the tower
his pale hands the moon
his hair whisp(er)s of smoke
which leave to join the sky
his glance becomes a CITY
his suffering turns to stone
his alien insides wander
until his movements cease

his image becomes your soul

— *@ Guggenheim Museum, 2/14/83*

side show @ coney island – Sun Ra meets John Cage

the pouring out of the pouring in
in range of sun   long &
guiltless

(pause)

in the chatter of the cosmopolitan boardwalk
sitting in humid air
of & of   ahhhhhhhhhhhhhhhhhhhhhhhhhhhhhhhhh
earth if not out
we cannot photograph triteness
of import
we seem to forget how to close the glass
traveling silent space ways argonauts
forget how to smile thru thunder
arrogant afraid
forget why we were brought here
moved from planet to mushrooming planet
recording fragments of tongues
& no longers

(eliminate heat wave)

a desert races thru these miles of light yrs.
choose a # remain there for an eon
do not wink @ pyramids
they are only the breast of mermaids
erupting
let dry skulls bear themselves
may their caps umbrella no more
the knowledge of sickened fingers

talk further of sunlight
read benches
lie still atop the waves

grow old & older
in the text & texture
of the seam
as brightness enters
surround your charms
with the child's pulse

eat fruit
drink fruit
open your mouth to the wilderness
the warps of eternal autumns
the white infused with voices & flags
meld the colors
forget
Eternal(s)
begin to dive to Rock

crisp delicious & fresh
crisp delicious & fresh
crisp delicious & fresh
crisp delicious & fresh
crisp delicious & fresh
crisp delicious & fresh
crisp delicious & fresh
crisp delicious & fresh
crisp delicious & fresh
crisp delicious & fresh
crisp delicious & fresh

magical realism

for Derek Jarman's garden

you burn the chair i sit in
your hat & glove perish with me in the gulf
engulfed by the tragic memory of your kindling

you rival yourself only in the stone & stream of circumstance
& a thousand times you cry from your enslavement
"SOY UNA MUJER"
don't worry i am no longer a child

my wick stays hidden yet somehow my posture invites your flames
YOU BURN THE CHAIR I SIT IN
& sit in the lap of ashes waiting for my return
your hat & glove return with me *your hat your glove (history now)*
sweep across the frozen cement
your hand brings forth the fire **you burn the chair i sit in**
the night sky flutters with *mystic* **smiles**
i sing a ballad to your muscles as you cry into the puddles *"yo soy una mujer"*
your scarf scuttles along the ice
your eyes skim the mountains of my frame i am storm & shield **yet**

You burn *the* chair i sit in *& the chair i sit in* BURNS
& your hat & glove & coat & shoes ride with me on my ride

& your scarf & your eyes & your teeth don't worry i know you are a woman

terezin man

i went walking
& as i walked
i found memories in whispers
& moments in cries
here on the walls of this
city

i unpacked my flesh
& lay it curbside
like a Beckett throw-away
& wondered where all the time
had gone

i bowed my heart
like a piccolo
bass
& fingered the hole in my nose
with the rough precision of
a weathered apprentice

i watched my reflection
in a noisy puddle
& soldered my eye
into a pile of
shit

shit
there beside me
in my bunkbed
memory
lying there always beside me
along the tree lined
walkway
walking toward the
bandstand

where the orchestra cooled up
tightening & loosening
strings
around their violin
lips
the arco forging double
S's

i went walking thru the streets
of now & then
& wore my yellow nite
like some vile innard
pulsing quietly below my
neck

& i sat
& rolled with the sorrow
& gave birth to a pillow
& the day grabbed me
with its serene stereo lusts
& i felt both forger &
forged
stranger &
founder
loser & lost

i went walking
in a land of barbed wire
angels
& red-candied dreams
12 years old &
ageless

going backward
yet never going at all

reflecting on my whereabouts
my origin
my name

walking forward yet circling
all the while
stopping curbside
to unpack my flesh
& wondering always
if
i'll ever
reach
13.

Mondrian's flowers

everybody
looks like a
tourist
on this picturepostcardday
with this
almost-paris lite
hitting 5th ave.
like the soft
hues
of
mondrian's
flowers.

— 4-23-91

Edouard Vuillard

a lot of life
in a little square
of white

we live to breathe
& breathe to live
our backs to the
audience
observing
the door........

sesamo

alone
or with others
the word
& the hand
make language
one is the other
& is not

eating sweets
& watching cherry blossoms
are like handshakes
& words
at once foreign
yet comforting

distant
yet warm

— Japan, 3/93

like wildflower

i look at myself in
your mirror
& am disappointed
again

the windfall
like
waterfall
(turned ice on my roof)
& my tongue like roses
frozen

picked me like a number
a birthmark
me   ocean of
topsy-turvy   canned
goods   empty &
obsessed
slip on your
pallet &
rust
your mirror
i look and am dis
appointed
        again

turn me over
& weave me like a
basket
with your ungloved cold
cold fingers
i
bottled up a
bottle of frozen
jissum unsolved &
wondering

ski on my hair
cut cut me
down like so much live
tart a
sweet tart filled with
weather

imprison me
throw away the key
no need to lock the door
i won't leave
lock me in your mirror
throw away the
glass

no one to skate on
my stomach   i am
jack lantern aflame &
gone out

ridicule my forecast

no one really knows how
crazy anyone
really
is

i suffer the reality of artists &
feast on the unlit
coils

a stove
white
its oven door open to the
draft
feet deep in the ice of a bowery
day
names burnt into the surface of

the ice
& the light that grows from the
branches of the tree
        is wet & smooth & hard
& clear

the pods of the jimson weed
are covered by near zero
temperature
they seem sick or
dead
they droop stem deep in the
no-thaw

skid on my face i'll
catch you with my
mouth

inside
the seeds are forming
unpassionately & will spring forth
& reform again

slide down my chest
over my hump & off my
ass
like a downhill racer &
i'll fall at your feet
while you save me with your eyes
& with crutches discarded
steadily
we'll lift us
with our arms.

joan mitchell

inside
the suitcase
there is
a
landscape

a photo
of a smiling
girl

a dancer
on
a
string

someone whose face
brings
only fond
memories

ludlow

(a college of geese)

we stand as monument to ourself
  glass shattered abandoned rock
        substation in turmoil along the river
human & alive or so we think & we are hastening toward
  the void created by the broken jagged windows
of all the factories on earth ground into soil by sun & rain

are we really breathing ? egg. lager. a hint of wind. college.

college: an organized society of persons
  performing certain common functions
  & possessing certain rights & privileges.

we are one town after another
cities within diamonds
big cons
empty beaches
fools that sing along the rails to prison
  no one to stand on the shoreline & point anymore
    no more joy in surprise

we are again we are
isolate & always in need of companionship
pearls on barbed wire
  strung across the rock
    where the solitary fisherman waits
  back here in some sort of harmony
  with armfuls of grain & electric

by the time i've had my fill my brother will be dead
his new house will be complete
his windows will look out on what will seem to be a vast wild & free land
he will stand by the water with arms folded & eyes smiling
then go back inside to work he'll be making all the right moves.

look — i tell her without opening my mouth —
the fallen leaves are climbing up the stairs —
don't bother me i'm reading a book
but look — i say — we've missed everything . . . . everything's gone . . .
there's nothing left to . . . see

a hint of wind. lager. an egg. college . . . . she closes her book & then her eyes.

we live with rats but don't know it

(Ray Johnson tribute, feigen gallery)

"... i do ... i do ... do ... do ..." —Ray Johnson

luck(y) struck she smiles
then they kiss on the $10 bill   oh! oh! (peso)
empty eyes illuminated by nite
   & the ever-present cracks of failed nos tal gia

      (take the f a i out of failure you have lure)
        (take the f u r e out you have) ... whatever

it's what we give to others / what we take from others

I'M CRACKIN UP

no matter
in the end we're all
water   anyway

all _ucked
            f
all ornament & destruction
all self
          down in one superior gulp

trains that stop & go & stop & parties
            (he liked trains & parties)
   & costumes &
                    bridges & piers
&   fears   all failures

all spoken out wordless toasted little ding dongs
thank you dear plaintiff my extraordinary little hunter
my scream my burning vein
my teensy-weensy spot of fuzz
my name thrown away way before my birth

(before you & i were born)
  (into this valley of locusts)
    (this golden opportunity)
      (this unyielding bareback rider)

the air is thick with talent
the doorway thin knotted air
come on
we're all just the teeth of trees
anyway

next time take off your clothes
put those galoshes back on

        (take oshes away you have gal)
  (take l e s away you have gosh)
    (take g l o away......)
      THE END

there are 20 in a pack until you open it
take them out /by/in 2s or all at once
all in all just smoke
we're all that / smoke
we're all jumping in
all looking for our balls in the end

& the young king cries BLOOD
wise precious droplets of
mouths / portraits / landscapes
still lifes / ice triggers / guns / or
other weapons
that drop onto his word-combing tongue
to form cubes of sanity
shoes that sprout from his lips
  & dribble down his chin

"sorry I'm all wet" — he says
me too — we're all ALL WET
all specks of skin
windows to be looked into luck-struck little ding dongs

(a termite lands on my finger
the car is ½ full
it's been raining all day
i try to shake it off NO GOOD
i tell it i am not wood NO GOOD i blow as hard as i can
you go where you must).............
THE END.

— 5/17/95, 9/13/19

co(*s*)mic

for Jim Brodey

all work done on premises.

i listen to old vinyl. but do not hear it.
look at books. but don't read.

warm. but i wear my coat & can't stop this junkdrip from my nose.
stuffy like the tune   he said i said but i said i didn't   (i get high but do not ingest
i know i didn't   low but do not sink)
it's all a matter of interpretation
any how   (fat & skinny had a race fat
                                                              fell down & broke *her* face)

        the buds   are budding   crocus-daffodil-hyacinth-tulip-lily
                                i prick myself on them all

mad & never knowing what at   this anonymous everyone you are.
i just keep getting phone calls that always ask.
a blue anchor that weighs down my heart
my heart   a white dot
white dot   with stick stuck thru it
crazy white our elders put us thru
thru chimney smoke and short sleeves
this is a weather of chance.

golden horns from atop our devilish heads   played on   this is our grace
                                                                our melody
                                                            our great big jones
my stuffy drippy nose playing with the cosmos
like mucus   there must be some relation   there
                    broad views   &
        narrow smiles
i kiss your cannolis but do not taste
smell your unsmellable snatch
a duckwall quacks my airy limbs   into place

my face   3 prickly pears yearning for a branch   (or a bite)
i'm branded art
i'm thoughtless garden
homeless trousers
the hole that shows your fleshy arse
narrated notes
i'm always being something in these pomes
friend unfolding
basic activity
long strides
heavy load

you can take my gal
you can take my soil
                    (i'll take   manahatta . . .)
you can grab my jack fruit
you can squeeze my mangoes
you can even establish my goals
make me a heathen
sing me songs
alter my language
rewrite my story
rain on my charade
explain the entire universe to me
(when our atmosphere is gone   the universe will still go on)
tell me there have never been any human scandals
straighten my tie
my mirror
my cold public smile
take away my africa
take away my america
weave my world so it's closer to yours
straighten out my memoirs   (or dictate them)
call me a clear blue sky
                    (mean & nasty like)
slice me til i drip
drop me like a hot dog down a narrow throat
                    (i'm gonna keep on talkin keep on talkin anyway)

jones /
dust / architecture /
ash
drop me like rain
like a sack of old. . . .
i
listen but do not hear
dump me like a dirty wind
(pushit don't pushit)
stress lingo honey i listen to old money
but do not hear touch
you can
you can you can youcan you can you can
rename my town
crush my car my spirit my spite my forest my mount
but please don't take away my eyes oh please don't take away my eyes
don't take away my eyes

a promise is a promise

(after a Derrida lecture in french, "littérature au secret")

Pardon — my world visible only to me — my world — an idea —
a secret — absolute as absolute as history the fool
& your direct reply only you know request
Pardon my month my active my passive — my exits — my "exists"
my secret elements —
too dumb for the smart kids
too smart for the dumb kids
some now falling apart like events responsibilities secrets truths
singular truths exposed unique edifice
grand moments with the ghost of language
the ghost of abraham ghosts in high office
skeletons in armor with swords fuzzy photos like forced necrophilia
poétique psychologique musique catholique esthetiques
politique mythologique logique alcoholique
at the core of silence in the silence of the atrium
abraham of the sky & the silence of the world a silence a silence
the silence of secrets the secret of silence
the big silence complementing the sword the tragic the standup
the standards the impoverished the children of ishmael pardoned
for their possible sins — imbeciles — noise reducers
reductive attractive distracting MAL
infidelitous lecterns movement
Pardon my paradox my undressing the precipice the mayor the
light the child the promise the sacrifice the respiration
the inspiration the expiration —
excuse my heart i cannot see it pumping the fool the cup of swords
the sour milk another savior — another femme fatale
Pardon — goodbye my solitary chair — my world visible as it is
to you only when an alternative to pardon is pardon is
conscience is lost in the field of her inaccessible
weave departs absolute the incredible primary weave —
the blue and the green and the white
chameleon like kafka excuse like kafka
familiar but foreign — like secret

like making a responsible decision should i sacrifice my son
should i answer the phone
should i show compassion
in an active or passive way

abraham gave up his secret gave up his freedom of choice & chose to
show his love of god thereby giving up his responsibility
— well pardon my fiction
pardon my difference my context my soapbox my "real" exposé
my mammoth situation my sacred text & machine
i am no detective no back biter
perhaps the secret of literature lies in our ignorance perhaps
perhaps this enigmatic secret is nothing more than a toilet stall without paper

Pardon — my request my reply my recommendation my not showing up
my facile façade secrets are secrets as absolute
as history as absolute as difference as different as phenomena
as manifest as baseball as attack-proof as atmosphere
par exemple what is the reason for kafka?
explain the lake & its reflections —

to respond to the cause to cause the response to confuse fiction
with fiction to exchange fiction with fiction you turning in on yourself
like words excusing the past accusing history as we write it —
incapacitated capacity example the marriage of two impossible alikes
the meteoric finiteness — then like entering a mobius the meteoric decline of
the giant squid for example a message from a friend during class the double
& its doubles the constant public excuses and spontaneous generations —
& after all a fiction is a fiction
& the bible is a story most believe

Pardon my father — Pardon my secrets — forgive my body's chances —
i am the evidence of secret
i am the difference i make
the beauty is in the beauty of the intricate
field on her back the news is just the news
pardon all the water & the words
the secret is in the beauty & the beauty

is pardon & beauty & sacrifice
beauty & absolute concern unconditional
demystification the democracy of choice
the responsibility of politics of text
the luxury of thought inscribed
inscripted within the position of mad mad love
L'Mor Fou MAD LOVE mystery to put the decision in the
hands of others to put one's liberty in the
hands of others making one's function the
sole responsibility of others —

YOU THINK THEREFORE I ACT

endurance

the sea & the door to the shore.
the sea of insight & blindness.
the sea & the door to the shore.

the sea & the door to the shore

THE SILENCE OF SILENCE IS SILENCE

the sea & the door to the shore YOU THINK THEREFORE I ACT

footnote: public culture art & function as edification
memories of a mongoose problematic —
kafka never forgave his father
did isaac?

II. NEW YORK POEMS

from *Subway Assemblages*

Godard 6 x 2

1. for Walt Whitman

rivers don't need money
but by my eyes
invite a crossing
sometimes
a queen
a problem
another alternative
all these things
before my
birth &
pain

like the world
is a crossing
sometimes
a river
for which we now use
a camera
to ferry our faces
across.

2. Borrowed Pens – Goings #1

at the end of the
world
there's always a place
to stay
            close to the line
around the corner

of dull transfiguration
grab the baby's eye
stop & let her
hand join yours

close is never
too close
nor far
at the end is
the center

fare as well as you can thru time & weather
the center close
not close enough
just go for it.

get close
at the end
it's your world
get close
closer
this close
at the end of the world between
subway cars she squats
& relieves her self

torn
go for it work
at the end of the world
just around the
corner
she squats behind doors
between cars

(((((the train slows as if for her))))))))

don't you wish you could
say that about yourself

there's help at the end of
the line
close
but not that close
uplifting & often
treacherous
varieties of help

at the end of the world
there's always
a place
to stop
& clean
the soles of your
shoes. . . . .

3. Borrowed Pens — Goings #2

he would
if he could
the father did
better than a clock

the man on the subway
with one leg
sitting
gets gobbled up

it isn't enough
to get there fast

it isn't enough

to learn

(how)

but certainly it is

special

to know . . . . .

4. Refugee Go Home (1st Trip Up)

(hi) story

your clock

or (h) ours

on a high horse

get off yours

already

would

if you could

RELEASE

on its back

(the horse's)

you're back

slide into the pueblo

you've never seen this much information

for so little

with so little message

never

a low rider

fallen

screams into his palm

hoarse

ly

viciously

painful

NO PAIN
IS YOUR
G AI N

Bill died
Tuesday
He saved
Lisa
on
Wednesday

your clock
or
ours
visions / in a hateful
form
that tax (es)
the fallen king

correct indifferences between the gaps in your mouth
your cataract eye
the fear & horror you produce
payless
for your trip to the mermaids

get back on your horse
fill out the saddle
& ride . . . . .

addendum:
laugh at the air
& the world
wave your swollen limbs

you've done too

much to

yourself

now

to cry.

5. Buenos Días (2nd Trip Up)

blind dog
buenos días
propose that you are
not
        (dead)
cannot read
                (will be)
                        ability to prepare
                          & exercise
                                    songs of the people

                                    beautiful songs
                          do not
                          be   raped
                            avoid
                                                            invite thanksgiving.

6.

        lumber

                                    sink
                                                s(l)ink

            (S) lumber
                                  a link
                                          however petite

kitchen

everything.

7. Life Net

like a ticket
to
paradise
i grab hold
at a(ny) price.

8. The Finale

i'm
church
i
declare
no tax
back
come
join
this
joke

Delmore Schwartz on the f train – christmas day

(the mind is an ancient and famous capital)

i sit opposite the **MIND**
to my right a couple sits snuggling
reading **AMAZING ANIMAL CROSSWORDS**
standing beside them
unshaven
broken zipper on a snapped up coat
a thin man with glasses
pale white
reads **WHAT IS A JEWISH JOKE**

"The mind possesses and is possessed by all the ruins
Of every haunted, hunted generation's celebration."

complexion   peeling   & discolored   he grins
   lips moving as he reads   chuckles from time to time
         chemical
                    searching for the light spots within   the dark
wanting to be feeling looking   younger

Delmore dead at 53
a clear beautiful discoloration
fielding every rotten thing
ever   said
about
him
or what he thought
was said
          updating himself like monument
                    instant
                    by
                    solitary
                    instant
                    briefly
            always only briefly

restarting
off
on the right
foot in equal partnership with himself & power
& history of this perfect puzzle world

from *The Superintendent's Eyes*

a superintendent's eyes #1 (from the basement of the academy)

1.

at the corner
from the corner of my eyes
a crowd passes

2.

you fine poets who live among universities
you glorious academicians
can you see civilization in your own backyards
in the ethnic eyes of the shopkeeper
buried in one neighborhood forever
dryly breathing
under a petrified cross?

the years have changed
but the times have not.

a superintendent's eyes #26 (my daily walk)

the shadow
thru the dirt-covered screen
is a man
walking like a shadow
thru a dirt-covered screen

how much space is left
in this document
this t.v.
digital groan

today is cold
grey
the sky is grey
the clouds dissolve
like a 20,000 yr. old
jawbone

i am a cloud
a jawbone

the shadow
becomes a pool
of dirty dots
the signature appears
on the
document
the promise
dissolves
on the stairwells

the stairwells need cleaning
again.

a superintendent's eyes #35 (spring street)

spring street starts on the bowery
& stops at the hudson
or vice versa

i turned down spring st.
from the bowery
toward the hudson
on my way home
turned the other way
as i saw you in turn
turn
your eyes turning away

the little girl said to her mother
                                        — *help me   help me   i'm drowning* —
    reaching out her arm   body leaning toward the curb

drowning on spring street
between the bowery
& the hudson

it is late winter or early spring
depending on how
you look at it

we dump our garbage
all over this island of dreams
& borrow what we can
walking
always
walking

you turn i turn

spring st. starts & stops
                              i always end up somewhere in between.

a superintendent's eyes #44 (the bard, ingestion)

sun visors up on his glasses
the black man
talks to himself

hot bright day
bottle in hand

"Anyone can read Shakespeare.
Ask New York University.
He can read Shakespeare. But she can't."

pointing randomly at people

"It's simple. Anyone can do it.
Shakespeare had no wife.
Never even had a woman.
A man can read Shakespeare
but a woman can't.
If the woman read it   he kill her.
Anyone can read Shakespeare.
Ask the universities.
Shakespeare. Nothin' hard about that."

the truck driver unloading his van says   AMEN.

we eat   & eat   & eat
we talk   & talk   & talk

chew chicken bones & steak   vegetables & salad

the cemetery is so quiet   the wind in the trees tears my wife in half

there is a moment of beauty   a cloud moving east
her face   & then   the close up

there's something too big here   too out of place   too real

a superintendent's eyes #53 (i hear sleeping . . .)

like berryman said too many of us have been born . . . . if i had it to do over again i wouldn't. not today anyway. it was the first big snow & i spent quite some time shoveling & salting down the sidewalk. if i did repeat this process, like snowfall, there'd probably be very little difference.

the big jowly woman at the table opposite me is saying something about sex & morning to the man she's with. the tunes coming over the restaurant speakers all sound familiar except they're sung in Vietnamese. the pavement out front has been breathed clean of its gift of snow.

i hear sleeping
& i know it's jump off time
i'm a wrapped piano
strapped & jacketed
waiting
to be rocked

a superintendent's eyes #63 (wisdom, magic & salt)

1.

i don't like bad guys on either side, he said, but at least if one shot you you'd know you'd be dying. the night crept cautiously around him. his eyes swelled with anger & excitement. maybe right then & there he'd explode from the magic of it all & his heavy breathing. maybe, he thought, if they'd only be more polite to each other then we'd have less problems . . . . . he started gasping for air & sinking to his knees. this at the end of that foul little triangle where Thompson Street meets Canal.

2 cops hung there watching the shirtless boys shoot hoops. as he fell downward his head hit the pavement & his 2 hands dropped from his throat . . . . . if only   if only

2.

in the refinement of place in the soft bellied notes that blossom from the thick fertile corpse of the land in the affirmation that i am still here though my body does not want to carry me my soft agitated fists only want to smash windshields & feel the godfucking wind . . . this is shallow fact & nothing else . . . . . hey you you there with the pushcart with the big square wooden wheels . . . sweet talk me out of here . . . haul me the hell out of HERE . . . . carry me to my conclusion . . . & you there in the chair beside me don't rub your perfume in my face . . . . . . don't ease your way into my lap . . . .

in the refinement of this place in the quick thinking of a good teacher
Lot & Thoth   will unite   will count
letters   learning   wisdom   magic   &   salt

when i own a club
all the glasses
will be
plastic.

a superintendent's eyes #69 (morning to sunset)

1. morning

it had been raining all night & i was worried. i promised
yuko a day of walking in the sun in search of signs of spring.
away from this neighborhood. i awake & walk into the kitchen.

drinking morning tea
rain
on the window ledge

after breakfast we settle down & try to accept our fate.
it rains & rains. the cats sleep. we listen to music. write. read.
sudden thunder. twitching. everything clean for spring.
i decide to mop the halls.

by early afternoon the rain finally stops & the streets
rapidly dry under a strong spring sun. we prepare for our
walk. the halls are clean. the streets are too.

by the park   across the street
blackbirds   quarrel

we walk for many blocks. new buds springing up
everywhere. the city, as always, sustaining itself. we walk &
walk until darkness & hunger catch up with us. the sparrow
rubs its beak on a branch. a squirrel rolls around in the
grass. how idyllic can things get?

"what a carefree existence they lead" my stomach grumbles

"let's go to that nice restaurant on 14th street"

she agrees & we head crosstown.

pink hyacinths @ sunset
breaking away from
themselves

we arrive at the restaurant, aptly named, SOL DE ORO,
very tired, order our favorite dishes, eat & digest the day. the
food is, as usual, great. we order extra rice.

convex moon
tasting a lemon wedge
her yellow sweater

we head home filled & contented. this big city night unfolding around us.

2. sunset (sol de oro – a reprise)

god must have stopped at the sol de oro. he must be there still in this airy space on w. 14th just above 6th ave. he dwells inside the menu & the smiles of the waiters. & guides the hands of the cooks. he is perhaps the final silent partner as he picks up our tab & closes las puertas de plata por la noche.

one rainy night
he must have stopped here
filled with hunger
& after whetting his appetite
he left a golden ray on this wide back street....

& for a small price we sit at the table prepared for us & eat until our stomachs burst
& our hearts balloon with joy

a superintendent's eyes #85
(my life as a storage space – *shadows*/writing)

1. bulk

null & void my fill exo-genesis
the body draped in flag archer
& the cross-legged beauty
pregnancy the experience of summer
  (prematurely)
rolls of undeveloped film swallowing power
degrees — unrelenting miles of cable
the missed connection software hardware
blankets & plastic bags
lps maps handtrucks books
statues chairs lineament lifelines
deadlines papers papers papers papers
tests aorta abstract real estate green miles
i don't know how much longer i can keep it all
it's time to learn a trade.

2. lightness

she says that shadows
look much better in winter
than in summer

i say the only time we
are detached from
our shadows
is when we jump.

3. the unbearable bulkiness of light

i was always writing like @ 19 in front of the mirror
on wood roses 3 days on wood roses staring thru the mirror

3 days at a stranger's vanity table swirling pinkblues
heaven & hell @ my shoulders like wings heaven looking
more like hell every instant a stranger's vanity
(heaven/hell) (bluepink) not knowing how to hold on to
what little there was of my self not knowing how to let go
                    . . . losses . . . trying to lessen my losses
learn from my losses hold onto my losses beyond the mirror
toes still playing like music the seeds as they enter my stomach
the poison as it enters my blood stream like roses
                       the blood as it leaks from my pen
roses of wood their petals as brittle as paper
                   their perfume as dull as my (t)horns.

a superintendent's eyes #89 (quartet for the end of time + 1 – food)

1. at a local café – here comes mingus there goes trane

i suffer from rediculitous — a sound & sore kidney with
a stone the size of a baseball where the old lady punched me
& a way too expensive but huge serve-yourself breakfast
where they call your name when the meal's ready in a
dressed down hick-style atmosphere in the heart of
greenwich village in a café full of "hipsters"
with beards tattoos & lumberjack shirts where ella nina billie
& monk fill the space quietly rising above the clatter &
chatter — but man these white kids sure can cook —
the maple syrup's hot & the bread's the softest i've ever had
                                        then the bad music begins

2. goat cheese & leeks (brunch) – for g.c.

i sit across from myself   empty plate
discuss the names of strangers
even those in my blood with a friend
discuss friend with myself
take out add on invisible sheet of a once blooming tree
have parts of my life stolen from me by myself
by friends by strangers that i do not even get to see
i am up to nothing i practice at being up to nothing
the sun is up in the middle of this
i pay taxes to the perceived of which i am
the same as myself   the empty plate removed
the glass   drained   the lemon squeezed beyond its content —

                        your ashes will go to rome
  my flesh will end up in a common grave if i do not act soon
i must get up & pay the check people are waiting
for this table.

3. at a not so local jazz club

in the dark @ the jazz club 2 guys in suits eat something exotic right down to the bone they suck out the marrow & wash it down with firewater you can see the bare white calcium shimmer in candle light — the flame itself seems like water sweating in the glass
"more people imagine the end of the world than the end of capitalism" — her words ringing in my head — the glass sweating — me sweating as dark arms in dark flannel with white shirts & striped ties whiskey themselves up — they eat animals that they barely tolerate — whiskey & bear — their animal intolerance of beasts — what difference does it make how we eat our ribs? the difference is the margin between the civilized & the uncivilized — a fork clicks against a plate — i am not nor ever will be the standard bearer of good taste or social etiquette though i consider *my* taste of a high caliber —
the pianist's fingers in the mirror & in real life are the only standard i can bear right now as he bares it all & i wolf down his music — it's a slow tune both savage & civilized — as the set comes to a close i slowly turn my attention away from the wildly civilized creatures in suits lick my paws with relish & enter the city of jungles . . . .

4. 14th street green market sequence

at the green market it all looked so good
i decided not to buy a thing
due to the warmth of the market i remove my hat & gloves
buffalo jerky "it's what the indians ate." he tells me

delicate small potato:
purple outside
as well as
inside

red radish:
sun
hurtle me home
ward

buy from a local vendor,
why? because
the country is right there
on 14th street!

i walk from the green market to my local super market & upon arrival discover that over night it had become something else. just like this neighborhood going from sweat shops to art galleries to trendy stores in a blink.

after consuming all these changes with eyes stomach intellect & heart i decide that i deserve a treat after all the hard work i've put in picking up trash fighting the elements & dodging insults & complaints from tenants & landlord alike. i head for a local bar.

5. scraps

julien,
i am alone in the bar waiting for my meatloaf
like my day & life in general i have been disappointed again
this time it's because they're out of mashed potatoes
they boiled up a new batch & have started to peel them
but the waitress says they won't be ready for an hr
when i arrived home today i gave the halls the once over
then called a dear friend
he said let's have lunch friday
i said fine until he demanded that i meet him in a restaurant
he favors in brooklyn
no way i said you come here   i wake up too late
it'll be a hassle going back & forth
& by the time i'd get home my day would be shot
the salad's arrived & i'll have to have fries instead of mashed

(ground beef   ground zero   daily grind)

anyway he said he always comes to manhattan to see me
so i should go to brooklyn to see him for a change
i said i'd think about it

& call him back
i never suspected that this was an issue with him
i thought he enjoyed coming into manhattan
& i hate that tit for tat social shit
the meatloaf's arrived & tastes very mediocre
& though i never wanted false teeth
i could certainly use some new ones about now
i've been constantly thinking about what **to govern**
meant way back when
it is not this country that is bad but its governing body
the bodies that make up the body doing bad things
for the greater good
i've been thinking about this for a long time
it's been happening like this for centuries
so i gave up voting ages ago
we believe what we choose to believe
what we need to believe
there is a greek chorus inside my head
& the meatloaf's darker than the night outside
& just as flat & uninteresting
language is an abstract thing & in the end there is only
abstraction & the words ***sorry we messed up***
since you are so aware of neglected poets maybe you will keep my work alive
after i'm gone that's if you find anything worth keeping after all i'm a poet
nothing more nothing less & i know what awaits me 'round the corner for
years i've been waiting & nothing's changed the flag gets filthier as time goes
by & the fabric fades & distance puts distance between things
but we should never be afraid of our dead
yet if there's nothing to be afraid of then why am i so afraid?
is it because we make war to take our minds off war?
the lady @ the next table talks about not being a great writer
& that maybe when she's 60 she'll turn out something good
& that that would be gratifying
she's tired of turning out yrs of schlock
though it's the most pleasant way to make a living
she's sad because when she talks to her friends back home
they don't get her
they're smart but can't grasp what she's doing

here in n.y. it's different
she's sometimes sorry that she's not that "other thing"
& that it's kind of ok to just be mediocre
& that that doesn't mean you can't change from one
to the other
vanity   ambition   everything enormous
the bar becomes so high   staggering   amazing
going back home
nothing
the man with her who apparently is the "other"
speaks softly
what's it all mean?
what we have in common is the mashed potatoes
what little there is to truly say
i sit on the fence so i can see both sides
but i've been sitting on the fence so long
that neither side appeals to me
so i'll rise so that someone can say   "he's arisen" or   "arose"
i've been pedaling the wrong way down a one way street
but then i found out   there were infinite directions
accomplishments   how did i get this far? the man says
coming back to that
i'm sure the mashed potatoes are ready
now that i'm done with my meal
i want to join their conversation
tell them that substituting fries doesn't work
i'd like to begin this all over again tomorrow
yesterday or was that . . . . . . i'll think about today   later
after decades of sinister plots   a sinister plot has been hatched
right in front of us   right out front   no lies right there on t.v.
those parts of our bodies   do not even try to hide their blemishes
to conceal their deceit   ashes mix with slick & we are fed
new heroes to bury
i'll rub the last piece of bread around the rim of my plate
to soak up the remaining gravy
ask for my check   & leave

L — steve

III. HAIKU AND OTHER POEMS

haiku 1966–2000

sunset —
footprints crisscross
in the sand

in complete darkness
he carries himself around
like the world

morning haze
only birds & cherry blossoms
awakened

the weather rides itself
like a mad painting
thru the day

there
on each iris petal
last night's rain

by the pond's edge
the stone angel
praying

hot red
azaleas
flooding my eyes

whistling in blizzard
my notes crack then
freeze in air

subway empties
3 young couples
holding hands

listening to blues
on a cold march nite
I think of changing my name to "sky"

damp march chill
doll's arm
caught in dumpster

early spring
4 black birds
on a barren tree

heavy spring rain
I turn my watch ahead

silence between
2 faces
the chairs

scooping up water
toward the moon
feeling the light

independent day
one wave breaks
& then another

sunset
the wave receding
meets itself

the moon &
the sacred heart
in a staring contest

as high as
we are here
the moon is higher still

pink roses
her lips
against the raspberries

they turn pages
I watch the sky turn colors

traffic & wind
my thoughts are the loudest sound

my breath on the mt. top
I want to carry everything inside me

(for my brother)

late august
perched on the birch bark
cicada's shell

early autumn sunset
green to brown to yellow to red

fish store
fish mouth o p e n i n g
closing

summer moon
between two reeds
the spider web

light snow:
one seagull
far from the sea

abandoned in snow
the stone saint blesses
the wall

on a lengthening day
I wind my watch
in the wind

late snow
ill fated
a pale half moon

blizzard:
old man's shadow
in snow

crowded train
my mind is a wind chime

snowfall:
one ray of sun light
on my tea cup

forest —
my origins here
untraceable

just another moon
no the same moon
Bashō looked at —

blue sky
blue fish
biting

sunset
untangling
the fishing line

(for Kaneko Tohta)

below discolored bricks
8 small bright leaves
sprouting

crickets
between stars
a silence

turning
in her sleep
autumn leaves

she reads
I read
leaves gone

******

again – solo renga

she reads   I read   again the leaves gone

clouds   move like tired old men
January sun   heavy chill connects my finger joints
"while I was sick" she said "the whole world changed
into a valentine"
again in a pizzeria   big band night fall
— Vo la ré — she orders a wine they do not stock

a different moon again no the same moon
Bashō saw many moons ago

face to wall
"Steve do you think god loves us?"
one big tear drop drops
in darkness . . . .

we walk again we stare at sidewalks

******

sanctuary
stars and rivers
forever babble

grey winter rain
I open my broken umbrella

squeezing oranges —
bird songs
on a cloudy day

late spring
fern's unseen
unfolding

monk on mule
my breath becomes
a zither

sudden storm —
the 3 pointed leaf
listens

big snow
letters disappear
into my new typewriter
frozen rain
dead leaves
rustling the moment

bleak afternoon
I buy Kafka's biography

sleepless night:
filling my yawn,
bird cries

mid day
holes in shoes
are freedom

storm's ebb
myself & waves
confronting

on my birthday
I call my dying mother

in music
in silence
a leaf
a leaf

acute loneliness
crescent moon
in a barren sky

spring moon
one legged beggar
embraces the coin

rose in bloom
man sorting
empty cans

cold cold day
feeling sad
I take a long walk

father dying
in the next room —
I spare the cockroach

crippled cicada
3rd day of my father's death

mourning dove
my wife calls me
to breakfast

rain no rain
today the weather
is like a piano

night garden
fireflies
in the cat's eyes

big dipper vanishes
morning becomes
an ocean of clouds

first snow
my shadow catches up
with me twice

paris moon
the sky falls
on my head

america's dream —
dogwood
in a gentle wind

sunset
an old dog's face
in the wind

in the bowery garden
all I see is
bird voice

dark harlem blue:
the house lights
go on

ice floe
sea birds
bobbing
endless field —
without paper or pen
I compose & forget

bathed in winter sun light
the old dog & its shadow

2 short haibun

after the rain

the tracks of a small animal cake the car hood, slope downward & slip into smudged streaks along the fender. afternoon shadows smother the old tree's bark.

chopping wood
I begin to realize
my age

as evening approaches, I just can't stop wondering about those tracks.

a parkful of winos

late spring
asleep on the concrete floor
2 winos

it is a mid-afternoon mug shot. the weather is sunny & warm except for a slight wind that chills the hands like the opening & closing of a refrigerator door. 2 kids are learning to kick a soccer ball around while their mom follows behind with instructions. they miss one wino by inches. his hair is grey & his posture fetal. he, like a bench or a small tree, does not even stir. he & the other drunk are like 2 converging tips of a goal post. 2 broken flippers on a pinball machine. too many similes here in a land where the wine flows freely. the soccer ball is kicked mid-park. children chase after it. i enter the dental clinic hoping that when i leave the pain in my tooth will have abated.

round & raw
the big yellow orb edges
toward summer

IV. MUSIC POEMS

from *Reaching into the Unknown, 1964–2009*

quicksand / shadow waltz

for Sonny Rollins

it seems beautiful
        but it can kill you
roar of the heart
      so low
within this bliss filled abyss
i sink
babbling
   irritated
      "oh ear. what you get is the heat."
nothing moves yet i am not asleep
there is a blue tray where i dream
of the faithfulness of love
eyes open
where i dream of future engagements
feasts
beasts along the roadside
playing seconds into my hearing
filthy
agitation
oh
sweet freedom
always seconds away
from this mirage of paper
   i am being buried
under
   this shadowy waltz
        within the hourglass

        desire flew
& my body disappeared
      "skin blood brain bone & soul"

grain
gramophone
gossip
& grapes
        disappeared
  & returned on horseback
      trickled away
like a side of beef beheaded
       then returned & wondered
"what's in a dream . . . a dream?
            what's in a dream? a dream."

memory & skin

(the David S. Ware quartet)

1.

his sound is linked
to memory &
skin
the hollow screaming that
skin does when lovers
in a dry sweat
rub against each other
hollow & full
his sound
filled with what we all have
beneath our skins
repeating memory
of body
reviving memory
of body
& then dropped

she drops memories on the air
they're forgotten
& gotten again
the way memories are
revived
like skin
hollowed out
scraping against itself
producing a metal sound
a vocal stab in the back
@ futures' end.

2.

cry a little
let water pass between

our skins
soothe the burning that sepa-
rates memory from word
heart from eye

we hang in air
circle each other
star & stone
death & life
for your serenity &
sanity
i close the door on
sentient memory
your glowing skin becomes
tree bark invaded by
nite moss
& i have already forgotten
your name
but it doesn't matter

he has a hollow sound
he wanders around the present
as if it no longer existed
& perhaps it doesn't
strangers call from windows
they cannot be heard
my lips feel like the skin of
a plucked chicken
i steal your tongue as it enters me
i am already memory
have already forgotten my name
a hollow sound
reminds us to forget what is
remembered
& remember
to forget.

as in my name is ....

for Albert Ayler

(with words collaged from interviews with Albert & Donald Ayler)

as in my name is . . .
flying around inexplicable as bearing witness having visions
as in the power of god miracle ghosts bearing emancipation
witness to the fallen
radiant array of . . . flying around piercing revelations
positions of touch
brothers & sisters developed free

i was born & my dad's wish for me was to be known thru the entire world
inclinations transmissions listening intently at age 3
playing ave maria at age 8
drink of the wine the fountains of wisdom
the forming of as in my name is . . . Revelation

i had a vision dark sky spiritual law illusion cleanliness
blood the true prophet
blasphemy discord true harmony perfection
make war with the lamb
& i was awakened to the kingdom

for me bop is a restriction humming new peace beauty
as in my name is . . . truth
marching conscious of strength of what we're talking about
music is good for the mind
follow the sound the pitches the colors
you have to watch them move you
have to watch them move   melodies going in & out of . . .
something you are left with something you can hum
as in to give peace you must have peace
music as a rejoicing a beauty going to happen do not focus on the notes
move your imagination toward the sound   sound to sound inside the music
listen to everything together it frees the mind as in find out more about yourself

listen to each other   free
not just free music but free spiritual music
hear the relationships of a free sound & know it's right
each person finds his own form as in you know what the next one will be
as in my name is FREE vibrato full force of life complicated textures &
simple tunes
tunes you can hum   as in HUM ME BREATHE ME   my name is World is TRUTH
is Fascination & enthrallment   My Name Is New
my name: Heroic My name: prehistory
search golden weapon saxophone   my name is nobody & nobody understands ME
nobody understands ME originality Song Sleep Scandal
desolation emptiness radiance
charisma interplay deliverance audacity ecstasy   the sound within sound
Nobody understands that i am trying to understand people praying healing
running after money waiting for the New Grass to grow but nothing happens
i should have left this place long ago hard obscure unsettling life
shouting & waiting for my time
hunger / success: the ratio of one to the other
the music > the riots it will not cause > the music
it has nothing to do with what people say the truth will set you free
march on march on
rejoice the sorrow the suffering the waiting as in dream
march on march on rejoice
as in one feels different things in different stages of one's life
the ARTIST's EVOLUTION Evolution as in MOment
to make the music new every time
feel the rhythm appreciate the music as in my name is response
responsibility chaos crazy impatience passion heaven foundation light
fusion dominion emergence force virtuoso witch devil saint ghost
circumstance abstract idiom cliché acceleration strength will
the ultimate capacity for imagination vibration mother father children
family myth courage collapse rejuvenation words &
words after all are music & music can set you free
& music can bring you peace
for in order to give peace you must have PEACE
that's all MY NAME IS MUSIC that's All MUSIC that's all.

John Coltrane

for Amiri Baraka, 9/99

John Coltrane
A bitter wind blows thru A LOVE SUPREME
& people are still waiting for the Ascension
with their eyes closed teeth clenched & fingers crossed

John Coltrane
old news is still news
assassination integration racism large schism & Africa?
is it still in Interstellar Space?

John Coltrane
the cicadas were buried in my head
long before I ever heard them
Kennedy King X
Kennedy King X
looking at the moon does not seem so strange
you do, John Coltrane, cause me to go on
wandering the Sea of Japan in my Bare feet
does not seem so strange
my language a thing of the past
the star fish & crab in their own universe
my universe does not seem so strange
I want to talk about I want to talk about
You

John Coltrane John Coltrane John Coltrane
i have taken the leap with you though the impression I get
as the Countdown approaches is that things are still spiraling
downward & are not, John Coltrane, made up of 3 Little Words
Where is the Promise — is it on Mars Jupiter Alabama?
Things are not what they used to be & yet they are
John Coltrane
My grandmother
it was said

sang her own kind of spirituals
while working on some underground railroad in a faraway land
Dear Lord Dear John Coltrane where are our eyes?
Can we open them on a Moment's Notice?
WAKE UP WAKE UP
John Coltrane
it is not we who live this LUSH LIFE
but Life Itself
as Death & the Blues
wait impatiently to follow
John Coltrane
what are WE Waiting for?
The consequence of compassion can be nothing more than
3 Little Words
these 3 little words that too many find so easy to say
Europa — Hollywood — Apple
do you think we will ever give that space? Have that space?
insects serenity joy
Are the Offerings we make all the wrong kind?
John Coltrane
were you living in the crescent of the Void?
can there really be Peace ON Earth?
do Dawn & Dusk truly intertwine?
the light's way up now
the shadows too
so I guess they do
we do
somewhere down the line
John Coltrane
always exploring new territories
I am there with you
my voice was mumbling about beauty
long before my lips ever moved

the world is in revolution
has long been in revolution
we've only to ask
the SUN

oh John Coltrane
John Coltrane
I haven't slept again
& I'm sure there are people out there
doing the same thing
barely breathing
waiting for the breakfast wagon to arrive
the air is electric with a new season
another drought has passed
another hurricane
I'm still here
though the cicada's time has ended
John Coltrane
some creatures suffer so long
for what seems so little
is there really a "GRAND DESIGN"?
what does a diamond prove?
John Coltrane
the world is a dangerous place
full of windex cell phones
& fax machines
women washing windows on windy days
comrades serving coffee on clear mornings
with the movement thru the trees
the realist music there is — shhhhhhhhhhhhhhhh
John Coltrane
it's all about good food & press passes
John Coltrane
let's not talk of torture or birdsong
of bondage or passage booked
i'll acknowledge there's hope
if you play me another solo
just play me another solo
play me another solo
play me another solo

patterns in a chromatic field

a far train
it is fair to say
it is
a far train
took too many shots
i lift a hand toward the beasts
no fit nite nor
that pc of cloth that holds my mother's *smile*

held by scaffolding i walk thru halo held by sliver of light
cement & brick wilderness
in a temporal sky of cloud & glass & heavenly blue on a mt of stone

across tarnished silver framed here within god's favor
held up
held on
held over
too many shots

shattered panes of ice along a street named royal
that now must end
nameless moments as temporal voices ask
where are you going?

381
375 698
475
608

SANCTUS

come sit at my table
we are pistols in this house of worship

slow moving

it is fair to say

even as the train awaits

us.

— 12/05-06/03, the historic st peter's church in chelsea listening to Morton Feldman's "Patterns in a Chromatic Field" (1981) – Ted Mook, cello. Eric Moe, piano.

Joe Maneri quartet @ barbès

(set 1 w/ Matt Maneri, Dave Burrell & Randy Peterson, 4/21/05)

1.

fiercer than tumult
quieter than noise
this untangling sound
a focus on brevity within a complex order
checked & seeing-eyed
black/tongued wherein belyeth
body's hotel
mind's museum
metal that forms the light
wood that dies for our joys & sins

bushed & dernam
this flat-manned roadway est tilled upon
rubbings on the dirt-white floor
glyphed beyond recognition
sentences untranslatable but open for interpretation
& discourse
ran this course
windows facing a wall preparing to be looked out at

irenam nosretep der nesor ein greb

epic destroyed by the friction of feet
a history of movement made indistinguishable
a treatise on walking   wiped out

we are so sad we can only hold our breaths
so enrapt we can only lick our lips
barely move our lips
as the wall prepares to be inhabited by our eyes
& the tales of migration are erased by our steps.

2.

this shadow is a speaker
its crooked shape waking in the light
a keeper of form
(s)melting into its own reflection

it's a hard-breathing day
this boy on the floor meditating
thru a language of heat & pain
reflection's shadow

an inaudible breeze on my skin
reflection & shadow both born of light
containing themselves within it

little troubles still seem insurmountable
to a cluttered & troubled mind
i stop always at the corner for a moment
then cross at the
light again

3.

OR SAY OH TELL
OR SAY OH LET LET OH HO
LLET YAS D'OR PEOP

OPEP HOT SWITCH OPEY TOH REE M
AR — (K)

RHAMEN(D) ROOD BONK BONK NEERGRID
EGNARO WOB DER
FLIMT

joy spring (riffin on Clifford)

for Bill Dixon

1.
the moon makes its own music
tonite
somewhere
music that seeks to constantly
interrupt itself
a piece of something already a part
of some thing
a grain of flavor
fading into grainless nerve endings
fractious parcels
sailing through the window
there
a view / a circumference
a broken piece of
volume
in the magazine fill the bucket
here
a rebel walk
i give to you / you give to me
whatever you give to me
tune yer ears
bowpie — ring oh the seem real
blue pink rose
this new street we'll call it
EXTRA PLACE.

2.
nite displays itself like a slain lover
whose bench was once a tree
slain lover cries / exclaims
I YEARN FOR BEAUTIFUL LANDSCAPES
there beneath the awning

yawning light
water falls — grapes
crush in the stomach
wine is born
i'm not sure where i am or
for how long (i'll love you)
some rain in the once empty chambers
of my bowels
all weird & strictly romantic.

3.
i'm a lucky guy
& can tenderly dream of
sunset eyes
knowing nothing about books or
prayers negative values
the symmetry of youth
desired placement
optimum opacity & ghost images

i am in the middle of a straight line
puttering away
exposed to the dark rocks
bright metal
dark trees
against an overcast sky
& the white-against-black mood
of the music
blind to color yet able to visualize
history's vanishing letters while
beholding agitation.

4.
the man from the forest
weaves
a clock of hammers
eggs tick the promise of how-good-it-re
ally-is aways

bell/wind of whispered flutters
echoesssssss pluralllls
a sense of patches
grand mar rocks the steepness
& you lie there
old & young / thinkers in a story of . . .
enjoyin yerselves
devoted to the limitations of the scale
& how to triumphantly overturn
IT.

— *6/17/10*

piano song

(Matthew Shipp trio with Michael Bisio and Newman Taylor Baker, cutting room, 2/9/17)

there are therefore
the reverse of reserve
a reverse revolution
a within the curl -E- cues
how response is given
responder taken
edged the clearing within the
well executed well presented
muddle
as in muscle or . . .
be ballad be broadened be
riddled
with answers that need
no questions
belonging to bathe(d) light
unalterable
as stage-lit the syrup here
the creamier melting
the ice here
cutting the nuggets
of sound b(r)i(g)(h)t(e)(s)
here
within this
wherefore.

from *The Mantis and Other Poems, 1966–2009*

after Cecil Taylor concert

sing not song but string tuned harp(ie)s-chords
lyric rhyme well constructed chaos nite —
now a room floats about us
enfolds & possibly loves us —
a completion to a still unfinished psalm.

let us lock the door & bar admission
but to the piano furious we shared with wet
excitement
let us remain locked to each other —

somewhere a heavy throated reed
wings above us & sings
not song but tight stringed well handled bass fiddle screech
let us remain in love lust & laughter
let us remain
let us.

— 9/66

the mantis

the furious Mantis
lets its claws unleash
        flower is spectacle & voyeur
the town is a multitude of tiny lights
flickering inside raindrops
        we are obese & greedy
the sting from his smile tells us he
                        is in ecstasy
            he flings his torso aside
                    & naked holes from the farthest worlds
                            shine upon his domed head

the Mantis is a cruel creature
that must never be harmed
for he keeps evil from our souls
tho our hearts might be sinking with names
names that are many but none
we speak only silence
watch & wait for the Mantis
to deliver its blow
muss up our minds
language us to wake, death & fulfillment
                                — soothing torture —
            rip the bugs from our stems
                        pick their wings apart
                            pull out their legs
                crush all visions

we poor flowers
tender earth-spent trees/
fallen leaves triggered embryos
the Man / tis grown larger   smaller
        screams into us exotic flights
                & bouts with all

Mantis is Mantis & we flower & bug
obese greedy
Mantis is the blade of grass   a great deceiver
who sprays a vocal-ease of everysound   at his tempered victims
rap/tiled
the Mantis is cruel — he takes evil bites off its head
eats menace & shits it into glorious fields.

— *carlos I, 12/18/86*

Jackson Pollock's early sketch books

the music posited
classical fire
eating up the angels of hell

muscles dispersed & indispensable
stood shook good hands
shaking
met
i'll never forget the night
origin
symbols sewn into our voices
                                        our eyes
                    the patterns that give up
breath   false   breath

pagan fire
hard heart
soft   wheel
turning   the camera facing the player's back
recording the folds of his shirt
girth of his strength
his muscles
the blazing melancholy

1st there was the breather
then there came the breath
                              the heat
                              the moisture
                              the sound
                              the thought
                              the gesture
                              the grunt
                              the drum
                              the spoke
                              the symbol

the word
the language
the tool
the chapeau
the whiskey
the hemp
the text
the structure
the shifting of bone
the art of the deal
commerce
war
burial
true   love
& the ability to listen

i   in the balcony
she   down in front
&   the ability to listen
the camera on the muscles of the mouth
the requisite self
a beach where famine sang

if i were a writer & you were a bird
i'd write what you spoke
every morning thru my sleep
even if it irritated me
sometimes
classical fire
the muscles posited & shaking
stood   shook   standing
handed the fingers beaucoup scenes
leaning on thought
my spokes beating like unmetered music
gasping   &   grasping at breath
still   smelting
still   wondering
still marvel   ing

still   searching
for the ability   to listen
to listen
beneath the sound   below the mind
to pleasurably grapple with the void
to listen to kinesthesia
to movement
classical fire
eating up the angels of hell
hard heart
soft wheel
deep origin
long breath
gentle strength.

— the knitting factory, 1/7/98

Cecil Taylor – Derek Bailey duo @ tonic

as if he were playing the music   on his skin

hair tangled   wire

case made   orange in black   orbit of choices

sympathetic cord   red   i   cu   lous   in conjunction with dynamic

snap this
the way wrists refuse to bend
as if my ears were the changes   addressed

don't make up what's right in front of you   hot   mustard   salad
BITTER chorus'   soured candy   broken   heart
not yet thru the sketches   & the scribe's already in my   BLOOD

feet of buzzards waiting in head
pounding eyes
saying Come to Me   come TO mE

(*wish i had*
a camera
that could make people real)

tripping over organic step
having less choice than will/string allows
incarnate
rooted in bulb

keep "I" out of rational choices
because museums allow such a thing

as if played the mass
your pockets full o' theories
the basic combination of movements

the eventual ride home
sealed walls   unhinged

if i never saw that face again
i would blessit take the juice away
& fleece the sadly rumor
but the time for invention is never gone
& thrives it like an old tongue
thru an intricate series of bailed canals

(*improvise within the Vocabulary*
of the particular language
you are using)

it's a basin in here   a self-created cistern of dark   was L I gh t   once
a bowl of delectable condiments
even now with temperaments awash & the whole meal sampled for FREE.

— tonic, 5/3/00

from *The Final Nite & Other Poems, Complete Notes from a Charles Gayle Notebook 1987–2006*

6-25-87

Charles Gayle Trio (Hill Green – bass, Dave Pleasant – drums)

@ The Knitting Factory

The Sleeping Tree

You
& the wind
        thru the young tree
                blowing
                        bending
                    screaming
                            wondering
& the wind outside
we cannot feel
& the ghosts
we
can
not
feel

the wind outside
that shakes the tree
young tree —
            the soul inside
            a willing tree
            that seems to go where you
        push it.

this was the first poem ever written for Charles Gayle the very first time i heard him play.

7-27-89

Charles Gayle – William Parker duo @ Ray Taylor's Living Room

set 2 poem 1

The Final Nite
or, Even Johnny Pumps Can Dream (for C.G.)

1.
don't torture yourself with incidentals
don't grasp your voice
& hold it so close to your heart
so that it sticks to the mts. of your throat
& causes you pain.

are your grievances & sins
in what has now become the birthright of us all,
a well,
a gushing falls,
that the kids i knew called "Johnny"?

2.
there are zebras in this living room
& men with strange lights emanating
from their heads
zebras behind glass
& eyes behind bars
in this order & function of ours
men with stripes & tears
in their pant legs
women with bars in their eyes
& fans from far away places
to soften the air

silks & perfumes

are not in the straw bag
alone with its shadow
& come from the dark continent
to hang on this shabby
plaster wall

there are tales to be told tonite
around Johnny's bust
& there is more than just a watering hole
in your horn.

3.
the blank space
in the heart of the t.v.
goes quicker than a gunshot
& for all the lives you've lived here
Rodney, Charles, William, Ray, Karen, Michelle, Stephanie & Jim,
there's always another life
another fury to call to you & drive you mad
another siren to sing you into
slavery . . .

& for all the lounging we do
& stealing we do
& giving we do
& walking we do
there will come a time
if the music stops
& the clouds congest
when Johnny & all the other holes
will be dry to us.

(note: Johnny Pump is an old colloquial for fire hydrant most commonly used throughout the 5 boroughs.)

set 2 poem 2

(Gayle)
he's screaming
for
tonite &

(Parker)
he's screaming
for joy
& he's tearing the heads off roses
& they are 2 of
the rarest coins
tossed up & slowly cutting the air
on
their paths
back down

(Gayle)
he is round &
turning around the
square
in a peopled frenzy

(Parker)
he is
ecstatic
in his need to climb

they are 2 cement hoppers
churning a vicious bravado
into the crumbleness
& speaking with . . . .
. . . . he's
& he's

& more than just thought
or politic
they're
accursed crusaders.

set 2 poem 3
—for William Parker

so i've become a doctor
now
i've cut the skin
from the bass player's finger
(excess hanging top layer)

he plays so hard it tore right up

i cut it with a small exacto knife
he held it taut
& i cut it

there were only seconds for recuperation
& bam
he went out there
& tore the strings up
second set

set 2 poem 4

Love Poem from the Woman's Point of View

he likes me in red
that's nice — so
i'll wear RED more often
especially when i think
i might
see him.

6-7-91

Charles Gayle, William Parker, Milford Graves @ Webo set 2

poem 1

the furious   the tyrant
the executioner
the stone & brick prison
lined with trees along the
highway of bridges
& dark confirmations
i walk like a stranger
like always
& always like a stranger
i talk aloud
to myself
only
& smile & say
how lucky i am
not to be
"one of them"
one of those poor bastards
trapped by social circumstance
& singing along
with guitar &
tape
in the tongues of their
padres y madres
who take control
& lullaby the
drunkards
into morning

poem 2

ok i say ok in the midst of my
delirium & the flanpatterned tile floor
in a mondrian whirlwind of uncomfortability
& soundsheets. ok the saxophonist plays in
front of a little black sign on a big white
wall that says MEN — ok i say
how far we've come these past few years
how far back in time
we've come.

7-13-94

Blue Humans (Tom Surgal – drums, Rudolph Grey – guitar with Gayle on drums) set 1 & Gayle Trio (Hill Green – bass, Rashid Bakhr – drums) set 2 @ The Cooler

lament #1 – sound drummer

she walks
with her
eye like auto
shutter

selective viewing

this
like a painting that
can watch only
one viewer
at a time

view finding

a painting by
an old flemish
master
making the best of the thin
hellish
light.

lament #2 – the shock

the doctor said
you were no good for
me

he practically said it to your face

to me

it was uncrowded summer Saturday
& he sat in judgement
like a caring father
and said
we should go
our separate
ways

we left his office
and grabbed and held each other's hands
tightly
as we moved farther
into the thin
hellish
light
        never once looking   at each other.

lament #3 – The Pharaohs

she came like
the white chocolate that
i used to buy on flatbush
ave.

she left like st. johns bread
she was that and indian nuts
too
    i filled my pockets
  walked my bike to the corner
    kissed my estranged aunt
  my mother's younger sister
                        & her younger daughter

rosella sheila
phyllis and paul
a whole family in my blood
their milton gone too soon
my aunt tied to her own tragedy

the afternoon did not feel menacing
as we exchanged quick greetings
in the thin hellish light

jagged lines of blues and playacts
coursed thru my veins
as i mounted my bike
broke my first piece of st. john's bread
& sucked at its core
she
still as sweet as
white chocolate
in the thin hellish light.

from *Long Play* (2009)

the duplicity of water

(Evan Parker – Richard Teitelbaum duo, set 2, the stone, 10/1/09)

aswash in the pedals
unwrenched & washed
clean-clinging frame
edge-soft lines sclatter
boltin' moo-like abirdin'

voices come out of box
  screen de/lights itself whirblin' &
wordlin' a long's anewdl
  framelit fram soft
spitlight caged in its own girth
        clean day

  add mirers & mirrors of mirth
worth more 'en evers
& em yes & sry me so why not bang
  the board & cry me a juicy circuit of
       gullivery
  circlin' even the river

      movement out of 4 hands
    playin' off the looker's sounds
        revved in the staytion airy
  perspective of hearing what are viva en momentum
         elec tronic ally *projective*

      battering softly
        on the strings of the whirled
          uncloseted & left to teeter thru a
             landscape of sound —
          then e(a)s(e)cape landscape & re-
               make

to phrase a coin much speculated pinging
& the cracking opens wider
& the strings detach themselves from
  their fingers & 20 fingers jubilate the sliding

    if at all there were a thing
    it would certainly be this.

evidence

(Evan Parker – Matt Shipp – William Parker @the stone, sets 1&2, 10/10/09)

for Baraka & Monk

germination
& the upper side
@ first dis en chant meant
chant as to sing
a slinking about core all sizes amonkerip(plin')
from solidities to amorphous blues line
fragmented   &   re-defined
low action plays diminished pianissimo
a rhythmic dynamic
reinventing the shuffle
as before gesturing hitched again
only the glisserials different & filtering
re-read demon/ends & kindly killers
a-boilin'
the progno an almost perplexed hesitation
& tremulous though not fearful
more thoughtful rapture
pluck upward the upright
& i'm waiting for explosions
sensation   inseparability   ratification
re-boost (sometimes we listen too well)
age(nts) of hearing / responding
jelly-hellos   discreet indiscretions
hey where's the whachamasyndromes?
what keen pinch work almost snazzadrople slapstring
upended granules / shepherding
& retinue of unwinds & playoffs
& again monkering toward the finish line
the evidence of histories combined
a second arrival
what others view at breakneck speed across the small expanse
i'm so weary of my language   this reworded miscellany
as the trio re-invents their lives on this day of the birth of 2
masters

i will take me down some
carry this weight to the river
turn on the gyrorator   underscore reality bites
& try to be less conniptious
  but first i must listen to the sound of the music
          (the music in the words)
   & bring that sound closer to my heartbeat.

so i had this dream

you and i were listening to some strange music
can't pin it down

my brother and father were there too
(sitting in some kinda armchairs)

sort of a weird out door almost surreal vacant
landscape
  (greyish dune-like)

all of a sudden you said to me
forget this music dylan thomas is on t.v.
there happened to be a t.v. there
& so it was —
thomas talking and reading poems

my father & brother
long dead
stared vacantly out
upon the vast grey nothing
listening i suppose
to that
vast strange
music
i was told by you
to avoid.

— after waking from a dream that had Evan Parker in it, july 2009

V. FRENCH POEMS

from *trial & error in paris* (2001)

trial & error # nature morte

bloated
floating in the Grand Canal
the history of a civilized nation
a boundless revolution
this is the tale of a young couple
sleeping in the woods of Versailles
homage to a real king
a failed revolution & a false
emperor
the water shut off so as to not disturb them

(fountains fountains everywhere but not a drop is spilt)

young Mozart played in the room next to Louie's dogs
little Mozart did his gig slept & split
she still says the sky looks like a painting —
after 20 yrs or more i haven't even cured her of that . . .
& the baths of Apollo hidden so deep behind the foliage
so locked away i must use forced entry to steal a shot

you can color all the poems you like
dot them with legend
ride your bike
pedal your feet
row your boat
along the Grand Canal
the great ones came between war & revolution
slavery & war
the advanced guard
they pointed reacted
got buried in the Hall of Mirrors like everyone else

welcome to my chambers
rest with me beneath this drab faded canopy

let's pull the drapes
& seclude ourselves for awhile
then we'll stroll the canal at sunset
beneath these low-flung clouds
this soft sky with its infectious light

the revolutionaries always
proceed the revolution
we must pay these trees for their perfect symmetry
buy a double ice cream cone
you know the kind
chocolate & vanilla swirl

(the young couple rises from their sleep)

in the Grand Canal
slowly circling
with
its dark brown glossy fur
its rigored paws &
bushy tail
Nature Morte
too close for comfort
too far to touch —

In & Out
In & Out
say what you like about the ripples.

— the grand canal @ versailles, 8/16/2001

giverny – trial & error # museum

i travel to Giverny for my father
who never heard of Monet
who never stood in front of the water lilies
& sighed
i travel to Giverny for Ryoko
who yearns continually to be an impressionist painting
an impassioned summer walk through a grand garden
on a Sunday afternoon
i travel to Giverny
despite my desire to stay in bed
despite my losing against myself time & time again
despite the changing Paris sky
the Eiffel Tower's tip
i travel to Giverny
in order to blur the boundaries between urb & suburb
tombstones & circuit breakers along the way
i travel to Giverny because she travels to Giverny
& because this is one of her dreams
& because we are so tired of each other
& the city streets we've walked for hours
every day   for weeks
& because she cannot go by herself
& because i cannot go by myself
i travel to Giverny on a train packed with tourists
tourists just like me

i travel to Giverny
with the thought of what i might be missing tonight
in some small club   on some back street
within the city's heart
i travel thinking about all the calls i should have made while in Paris
all the letters i didn't write

i travel to Giverny   for my mother
who sometimes wore dark glasses on hot sunny days

who never stood in the museum garden muttering to the bathing statues
my mother who tried her best to give me a bit of education
outside the system   despite her own lack of knowledge
my mother who loved me so much it hurt
& me not knowing still if to love means to inflict pain
i travel to Giverny on a train filled with proletarians
who   like me   i presume   are traveling to Giverny
          for the first time   for themselves
& for others who will never make the trip
we travel to Giverny as the landscape changes from urban
          to industrial   to suburban
   green white collar like Long Island
                              we'd sometimes visit Long Island
                                        Giverny
          i feel like a train wreck   &   she feels blessed
& we concur that ignorant does not mean stupid

i travel to Giverny as the clouds & sun vie for equal time in the tooblue sky
          to Giverny   to experience someone else's life
a guy   just another guy   she admits
GIVERNY
the genie has been released from the bottle
& it's just another guy
a dead guy like my father
who puts his hands behind his head
closes his eyes & naps
dreaming about the colors he used to paint the walls of strangers with
the neat colors that become indistinguishable strokes of paint
the strokes becoming lilies on a faraway pond

i never asked my parents what they knew
or what they'd seen
small yellow wild flowers & Queen Anne's lace along the tracks
i never thought i'd meet someone like Ryoko
with such honest   romantic   simple   & unfulfilled desires
her frilly hats & flowered dresses fluttering in the wind of her kitchen

i travel to Giverny   for my brother   who travelled to Florida too often

i travel to Giverny   to Giverny
for my return ticket to N.Y. is not for 10 more days
& my return ticket from Giverny   is for tonight

Giverny
G-I-V-E-R-N.Y.
Giver N.Y.

i travel to Giverny   for everything I have is in someone else's hands
& everything she has is in someone else's hands
& everything he had is in someone else's hands
i travel for   my father
my mother
i haven't even got there & the journey's wiped me out

i travel to Giverny to Giverny to Giverny
i travel to Giverny to Giverny to Giverny
to see what i can take back with me
to see what i can take back with me

phenomena of interference (2004)

today
charnel angel arose
& offered us a ticket to the PRISM
we arrived in LIGHT whole bodies
embodied within the ORIGIN
turning into mirrors of water
facing a forgotten sun

the sky is blue concrete melting into traffic
the window is invisible
we enter & wear our ligaments like a coat of arms
legitimate heirs to vegetables
origins in search of Origin man rotting / within the absence of
color
tho nothing is without color as
nothingness itself in B&W is illuminated by its primaries
Bio-logic the politic of color *elected*

from the tip of the candle to its base (nothing is in simple b & w
tho the DARK is so difficult to penetrate
for the dark contains all that it is not)

impenetrable — unfathomable — GEN — beginning & end
yet the borders of darkness remain always in light
"*light*" i will not say "*light*" as i plunge into myself & awaken
turning away again turning into again
l'ange debout dans le soleil at the edge of the sea
where the light is invisible yet the dark is a visible light
where there is no light but only light
is where it is within the courtyards & archways & across the
passages of dream
"*dream*" i will not say "*dream*"

she dreams amongst the rich blues & pinks
the earth-encrusted browns the sleeping blues & pale yawning yellows

obscura

(m)orpheus   resonance   sequence cadence absence

never an absence   always here on the green planet
it's about the effect of the sun on the tangled vines
how we live within the light each day
how it blinds us w/its vanity
coaxes us w/its madness
maddens us teases us
leads us into nocturne & fire
invites us embraces us
makes us feel safe
& abandons us
i will not say "*safe*"   play SAFE

ego is a dynamic lamp which overshadows the moon
the moon is a transparency
a false light
a mistook hope that only seems to guide us

do not be misled by your reflection
it is not you
it is a cloud that swallows knives whole
& offers no resistance
it appears as charnel angels
appear more transparent than
dream than light
it offers you a ticket to view yourself
but cannot guarantee your journey beyond
the stop requested
it offers safety where there is none
it is magic that makes you think the
trick is easy
then fools you again & again

this light this disappearing angel a finite clearing

Regulus/Sum/cup of Light

study for a fugue > complex sentence simplified
the furniture of decision
HORIZON —
a spilling over as in vertical
i will not say "*cup*" or "*runneth*" for that matter or....
parallel needs
perpendicular desires

TACHE SO LAIRE
The problem of color is:

the eye is a glass in a wooden box
is a
STOP SIGN
a universe
a wooden leg in a glass house
an apple changing as it ripens
a decadent drunk
a gentleman
a woman of sir cum stance
a filter cigare(gre)tte
the seasons
the way the colors merge
(M)ORPHISM
turning to look one last time
before leaving the system
"*system*" I WILL NOT SAY
HELL synchronismos
new tones
musique i will definitely not say "*music*"
or "*glass eye*" or "*seasons*" or "*soul*" or "*angel*" or "*river*"

the angel arrives at the river
rather rivers of angels arriving
are rivers
reversed
partitions
part

notions
the color of bowed rainbows

i cannot believe i said "*rainbows*"
w/glass eyes &
souls
made of
seasons

the interpretation of song

I WILL NEVER SAY "*song*"

allegros *andantes* *finales*
CORRESPONDANCES
secrets refract ures
where
white reflects & black
absorbs
the sound of color
the color of sound
where thought forms
& voice forms
& sand turns to glass

how even in LIGHT there is darkness
even in DARKNESS the light

(*did i say color? did i say sound?*)

from *assorted poems* (2004–2017)

the island of Gustave Moreau

in a time of beasts
there is the beast who knows not &
the beast who knows &
the beast who knows
he is a beast &   the beast
who knows he is not

Gustave Moreau was very fond of monkeys
& their closest rival   humans
particularly   women &   angels

oh, he also enjoyed lions & elephants
not to mention   horses

"what is the law?" "NOT TO EAT MEAT — that is the LAW"
"what is the law?" "NOT TO WALK ON ALL FOURS — that is the LAW"

(rising in a room full of light)

upstairs w/the big windows   where there is no light

"what is the law"   to wake up in the morning.

— paris, 2/25/04

le corbeau et le courbet – for Ted Joans

today the light is so bright
diffused light tracing det snaoj
life a backward shadow
@ the origin of the world
memoir of a pr. of bronze balls
too cold to fuck along the insane river
where the rhino dwells / or say hello Mr. Joans
as the sun writes these shadows on my page
facing his face privately @ Le Rouquet
where all's o.k.
& the madame you spoke of in your pomes
still receives l'addition
as i subtract nuage your hand wrote each
curlicued exquisite corps/e
(dis arm me o' poésie accursed)
while the bogus suggest how others should play with form & order
on Rodin's aching back

(B a l l s AK)

the 2 young femoiselles actually ask if we mind if they smoke
i say "yes but it is not against the law here"
wishing now we sat with your NO SMOKING sign
to shove into their pretty faces
as they proceed to pollute their lungs & ours
as we sweat on the opposite side from where you sat every day
as my overpriced café crème arrives

Mr. Sun begins to move behind the blding across the street
as Mr. Slick & the politicians shove their dicks into the mouths
of the people & i wrap my mouth around my omelette parmentier
& Mr. Sun disappears as you would

leaving its reflection behind as you would
leaving its mark on the street as you would
spreading its soft lyrical light here on St. Germain

& i ask the waiter "did you know Ted Joans — he sat in that corner there"
pointing to the far end of the café
& he says in french "yes he's been dead 2 yrs."
as we both simultaneously raise 2 fingers
& i say in "frenglish" — "he was moi gran ami"

& as he cleans our table i stare across the light stained blvd.
at the fancy soap shop remembering the little mouse
she & i saw scurrying frantically about in its window one
warm dark night
way back when.

— café le rouquet, paris, 1/30/2006

Goya

moonlight thru the cracks
sunlight thru the blinds
he died in this city of white windows
what was he thinking aboard the ship?
what was he thinking as he crossed the bridge?
his stomach began to sink
his dreams fade
black was all he saw
what was he thinking as he turned back toward
the shore?
watching the ship sail away
suddenly realizing that a dream was
only a dream
a dream of spices
where slaves never cast their shadows
but where their souls were bought
& sold
a white city of wine & oysters
where the clouds rushed wildly thru
the moon
did he puke out his dream
vanilla dream
chocolate dream
peppered with cardamom & paprika
what were they thinking these exiles?
were they dreaming of status &
parks?
were they inviting future
revolutions?
were they wishing they could sail
back home?

— bordeaux, 2006

Diderot and me

1. paris (me & Diderot)

on the bench between me and diderot
a bearded drunkard   then another
sacks of wine beneath their eyes
between their eyes
broken bones that barely contain their breaths
dying of rot
quickly one rolls a cigarette
looks down at his shaking knees then up at me
the bus engine replicates the polluted engine inside my skull
mad science rules our lives   mad men
    questions & responses / leaders who are misled
        peso / blanco / hot
  denis d wears a wig of pigeon shit
          son pressed against grief / deluxe saliva
        another nice servant stocking up on provisions
          in an age of sellouts and soldiers
          no different than any other age

  let me lead you thru the world MON CAPITAIN
let me guide you through these volumes of descriptions
              we've created.

2. new york (thru john ashbery)

  come back
    after the warning signs have chilled
      in a few days these days will be over
        lists forgotten just like that
          fist-filled dark alleys at year's end
            fever rising in my peppered loins
              tho no more blooming told
 simple scant light within the interior of my embankment
  retrieved undercurrents   uncontrolled noirs
        at the new frontier

& still to some it doesn't matter
& still it only matters to sum.

— paris, 2/1/07; n.y., 3/27/07

the cherry tree in ivry

we walk down victor hugo to where it meets molière. *SIT'AS SOIF* — to the old bldg & the sad little park with the saddest benches i have ever seen. all filled with emptiness. past a rail yard of empty flatcars. remnants of sand & gravel where chimneys spew empty smoke 24 hours a day. she is still obsessed with dead people, for instance in this reconstructed town where Artaud spent his last 4 years pouring himself out the way only garbage eating incinerators & madmen do. incinerated himself after the close of another great war & so close to paris. the overbearing fig tree suspended over nowhere bearing all its inedible sins. she dwells inside dead people even as the air is being swallowed up by swallows & startled by starlings. he must have walked here beneath the still moving hands of the clock in the empty window of the shattered clock tower. it must have been so different then. his life an imaginary landscape. homo economicus suicided by a singular capitalistic enterprise known as INSANITY. *spebi spebi exquisitum sito sito ten/nees sinnet sinnet octortu* — casting caca spells on the world — past the bureau of activities — down rue pierre semard where . . .
within a space of nowhere a full blown cherry tree appears & perched there within its dense leaves 2 unkempt brothers in need of baths. almost grafted onto the branches like misplaced cherubim lost or fallen from heaven & replanted here in the arms of Babylon their grimy hands cupping untold numbers of cherries.

as we pass beneath them one brother leans toward us
& offers us the sweet sweet fruit filling our empty palms.

empty courtyards. empty parks. empty benches. empty cafés. empty tables. empty bridges. empty factories. empty houses. empty warehouses. empty lives.

best cherries i've ever eaten — she confesses
as we spit pits onto the empty street.

postscript: here blood sang blood a chant of liberté d'espirit un poem authentique
un grand partage incomparable amour affection imported diverted indifferent
la machine that sang & sang & sang.

— *ivry-sur-seine, 2007*

2 brothers (complet) — for Vincent & Theo

2 brothers side-by-side. 1 having fed the other for all their short lives. total solemnity. 2 brothers from the northeast. 2 rooms 30%. 2 brothers. had they ever discussed politics? by their time dying months apart. buried in a country they loved but that was not their own. there were presidents & other elected officials proportionate to the population. 13% of independent ideas. windows where mary's light shone thru. covering the land with freedom. *"how are you?"* she asks. *"i'll ask her."* i answer. of the self populations fine voting boxing pathologies them selves laughing about outcomes. these so good. so filling breakfasts. okay. can anywhere beat this?

1 orange pressé
1 café au lait
1 tartine (with butter & jam)
1 croissant
1 plate of scrambled eggs with ham

---

total: 9 euros & a backfire a view of the museum activity always quiet corner unlimited seating time discussions about market research joint ventures joint capital putting things together > 2 brothers > 1 fed the other > a regular corporation > a real business > 2 brothers had a real business. 1 supplied the goods. the other the money. both liked to eat. 1 scattered himself around the town like streamers in the wind. or stood stationary as a target in a wheat field full of crows. did they discuss who might have been in office then? did they ever go to a concert together where perhaps 3 singers (women i think) performed & at least 1 of the singers singled out 1 of the brothers looked him in the eyes while her red lips moved. the corners of his dry mouth curling into a slight smile @ her touch. did they the 2 brothers ever watch a bullfight together? bullfights being so unfair the way elections are. did they ever see the cliffs? i did yesterday. i even stood in a cave for awhile. did either know what was about to happen? the way bulls never realize that their spines will be punctured before the fight. lousy picadors darting about all armored. 15 minutes to kill. is this what our ticket was good for 3 hours worth of killing? could the brothers even endure sitting through the first killing? their fertile minds turning arid. their time together a brief opportunity to speak in their native tongue. next to me a true traveler speaks about the elections & the middle ages & butterflies. spring is an unconditional unpredictable replay of itself. let's go somewhere else tomorrow. somewhere where sunset begins @ 7 P.M. & not 9. so many events go unlisted. so many lies unnoticed. here i slept & here i will sleep again. a growing archive. here for every day of my life while i am here i shall remain to some extent HERE. i will not leave remnants of my breakfast behind the way the folks at the next table have. & i will try despite my many shortcomings not to be like a worm crawling out of the mouth of an infested BODY > *"my mask is no good. art no good."* 2 brothers lie side-by-side. a small cathedral covered in green. a bouquet of near-dead sunflowers close by. a sickening homage. dark moist black centers heavily veiled doorways. a reflection of a tortured love this perfectly clear afternoon. keeping them company until the rain arrives was a tip included in the check in their day? did either ever eat an omelette naturale? discuss truth? did the brothers know there was such a place called texas? did 1 brother say to the other in a fit of laughter or a moment of pain or delirium hands trembling *"ah. it's you dear brother. just point me in the right direction & i'll show you the WAY"* ??? OUT.

coda: as blue does in a one star night sunset smashed against the window or as micro leg-ons in as seen of opal lapolos craves a newance as newsance in a sense thru godheads & kingdoms & hearts torn out boldly offered to para/dice a pair of diced ice eyes . . . the way a sparrow wanders the restaurant resting here restoring there run(t)ling crumbs & folded flies gets out of reflex the way storm rise follow down red fringes of remainder & only minds drop on the ghost's flesh singeing the do to a small spot on neckline agasped & pale shadowed on the wounded floor typo cross patterns where kings & queens & other parts of their (w)holes ar put to rest & chas(t) ed down this stubborn day into door/light

history > yellowed paper reading the score what is left after everyone else has left a replica of a flame a useless tower spirits lost in a crowd somewhere stretched between adolescence & childhood the accordionist's last chord & a world fueled by money & wanting

what is useless to one person is necessary to another. what will be left behind?

— le cavalier bleu café, paris, 5/19/2007

for Rilke

Billie Holiday singing
Night and Day
in a bar on rue de rivoli
the sky so dark night & day are
indistinguishable
the place des vosges a stark square heart that repeats truth
the way a calendar
begins & disappears

bizarre how the old synagogue
shaped like a torah
repeats with its bearded eyes leaning out the window
the eternal sources of illuminated vaults
rarely open to the public
where day & night
are low slung clouds that rush by whispering "no more spring to drink from"
here a koran filled with sacred warnings unravels
breath held wide open & embryonic

& from the bottom of a chasm
where night meets day
& mystery is the only light to read by
i look into torn works parlor games &
the rubber rooms
that hold my thirst in check
& proclaim to myself
quoting an out of season (b)ramble
"Behold I am alive . . ." a "surplus
of existence is welling up in my heart"
where Night and Day become one

— paris, 2007

poem of love & war — After August Stamm

1.

sun radio
in the imagination of horrible war
parallel to ridiculous
hack-in-credible fix of brutal sarcasm

2.

merci, merci, mercy shrapnel grenade fuselage
unparalleled courage / just cause

i sit in the parlor awaiting your return oh, atrocity
merci humanity — understand?
the person — the bell — the armor — the looking glass
devil language — universe of death —
the horse — the mountain
(marching marching)
new expression & day & its limits
& space & its triumphant conscience

without extension or dissection or conscience
what is left? brutality & company & destiny & exquisite magnetism
man woman sun fresh air & love my love
as it prospers projects transforms into letters friends messages
thru eternity
mon amis companies plural(ism)s foundries
what is left of a tired country & what continues to reason in this floating world
marching & marching & marching & marching
& tomorrow our terrible love resumes — our horrible love resumes
our love our lives with our fatigue within this internal & shattering
WAR
of
CADAVERS
to aspire within this infant hunger that consumes me
devours me
to expire & be a corpse of flowers

a forge — a force — a strange grenade of combat & love
that so quickly is obliged to forget.

3. enigma

after the storm
a rose-pink sky bleeds
into the trenches

— paris, october 2014

the final VISION – the cathedrals of france for RODIN

(Anselm Kiefer exhibition @ the Rodin museum)

key for the eye's glass emulsion

tho in / stability
the *E* / motion of ephemeral materiality
flat as movement is flat
fat marble egg weighed down by its un-hatching
her disembodied arm / its fingers of detached enigma
his later to come
an example of inspiration's samenesses
amongst the intentionally broken DATES
times running out & down
p(l)ast/e (o)r (al)
deliberate un / intention
hol (E) i — ness
but there are those rusting cathedrals
dismembered towers
leaning into a sea of peeling tar
like dinosaur jaws
reading the rotted sunflower's BOOK
unable to turn those massive pages
such miraculous decay of perfection
the assail(ient) time-frozen dRIP

NE PAS FRANCHIR > do not cross over the LINE > its ***weight***

those pretty naked girls lounging far from PIGALLE within the cathedral's hart
like day & night or one's arrival in HELL
here in its midst where Kiefer mirrors Rodin's seductive nakedness
the heavily delicate nakedness of watery young flesh
pale orange pages of flesh
w/his own more obvious attachment
& self-consciousness / the consciousness of stones
& the marble maiden whose life exists in the veins
the (un)harnessed (M)OLD>

a BRACE to hold one's tortured shape
the broad foot
& probing dismembered HAND
the death of branching armies
"climbing toward the heights"
of the ABYSS
the well oiled palm OPEN & ready to accept donations
the VALKYRIES' quiet trumpeting
that 7th note
always the clearest memory of creation

& in their finality
the worker's stiff overalls
of plaster & paint
stained white
as some think death might be stained
hanging beside the young girl's frock

& she, (*SANS TITRE*)
with her dry cracked earth/mouth
& empty eyes
that gather in the STAINED glass,
breathes patiently
waiting for her father to return

waiting for the moisture from the LIGHT

—paris, 10/8/2017

VI. LATER POEMS

the big dipper

for Steve Cannon

it was a long time ago
but it seemed like only this morning
that i lost control
of the air
that i needed a wake up call in my veins
to scour my blood & start my pulse
to move my life from my fingers to my heart to my toes
& back again

early morning   as clear as can be
the strong wind moves against me
as it did last night when i tried in vain
to point out the big dipper to anyone willing to look up

last night when my blind friend said that it was 40 years since he started
50 years since he stopped
started stopped started stopped started again 50 years he laughed
& said cope you can cope with it & i said cope you gotta be kiddin' cope
just so damned afraid the dope'll kill me before life do
falling apart everywhere but the center that's all

it was long ago this morning as the late spring wind
led me to the waiting room
where bodies with tired faces stood
& flowers fresh cut or otherwise were nowhere to be found
i listened to the air control valve open & close around my fingers as my ankles &
thighs no longer felt like a work in progress but still a work in progress none-the-
less feeling like if i haven't woken up by now i never will feeling like naive is not
such a good thing to be . . .

maybe 4 other stars besides the 7 in the dipper were visible
& one needn't have strained to see them.

"i want to escape . . ."

(Robert Frank exhibit @ scalo gallery)

—for Gregory Corso

good bye
hope
unclear nuclear hope
good bye
volcanoes fish experts
UFO's & foreign lands
good bye elections
& election fraud

good bye fantastic operations & sandwiches 5 cent penny candy motel rooms with windows
good bye
palm trees daisies & ideas
dark silence music & the past

good bye
ode pretty girls birthdays hrs. minutes months years
calendars good bye seconds
ruins
photographs of ruins
coffee cups
coffee
tea cake
table
spoon

good bye
gesturing space within emptiness emptiness within space
good bye
blooming concrete acanthuspaperchristmas
good bye
daddy blitzkrieg truth & dark silent music
shadows

good bye
crowded rolls of film hanging like fly paper in a room occupied only
by your ghost
the image of winter
perched upon the sill of my eye

good bye
you streets that i know of my youth middle age & my demise
good bye
you that i have never known will never know & have forgotten

good bye ***BELIEF*** *medicines & painful conditions*

good bye
weather postcards differences travelling & visitations
good bye
inventions adversaries & inventory

hello to nothing

good bye preparedness distance deception & necessity
small talk big talk people who are gone

good bye to tributes

good bye images bullfights speed blinking images & unbreachable
entanglements good bye vocabularies purple potatoes
& holes
good bye therapy exercise visitors disaster & you

good bye to you to how i look at you

i want to escape have to escape need to escape to escape escape.

— 9/27/28/00

subway systems

i have a double life   the homeless (sha)man said
there are 2 of me
i have 2 selves
i never use them at the same time

i live in double time
i try not to make it a habit

ny is my nightmare   my dream
it is what is beneath the tracks
defiled virgin whore
maladjusted trans-sexual goddess
cross-eyed cross dresser
homeless shaman as greasy as the tracks
i am consumed by jealousy   he says
it is my job to carry this burden
so that you do not
ny is skeleton & frame
heaven hell tributes & lies
the facts as he sees them
skyline & light
city of fallen angels
extinguished stars
ny is nature morte
landscape & EATS
jesus & buddha & god
ny lives on borrowed digital time
like shaman
leading a double life
the good the bad
the epi-centre
outside the centre outside of time
a part of & apart from america
what is beneath the tracks
shaman living on outside time

ny is 2 selves
never the same thing twice
never living together
as to not use each other up
body soul
ripped greasy ugly love
ny is what is beneath the self the self the other self

— 3/30–31/02

the portuguese letters

first letter

in paradise astonished by the resistant mountains
she in tight frock & turmoil
confesses; my Adam   in the dark world   despair   insanity useless longing
my own desolation   i perceive   your indifference
shame   neglect   betrayal

i gave myself fully nothing left
the altar candle burning to its   bottom   my sorrow bottomless

in my room confined   within the heavy air of your LOVE.

abandoned

second letter

if you suffered in the storm
my stormy suffering
is thrice
my concern for you boundless
as the sea

pain delight passion
exploited by your gentleness
i swayed & swooned   like a ship
tricked by my desires & by your limitless grace
tears sighs   miserable death

born to this   to this i stay   blind leading myself toward sleep
awakened &   nourished by your cruelty.

horse rider hate honor surrender my court martialed heart
would that i could tear it from my chest deserter that it is
& dispatch it to you as remnant.

i see your impatience
here take it and be gone.

third letter

she wears her words like skin
her skin thin as the parch she writes on

you hold me in your hands & read me

she can no longer separate her love her hate
her complaint her suffering
tyranny of the senses despair
his eyes she addresses them from the balcony
they envelope her she is stamped & sealed by her longing
her poignant flagellation
oh poor woman insight shortsight cruel separation violent search

salvationfateinflicted tears ***i wait for my heart to return***

fourth letter

returned to reality yet so removed from it all
i envision your escapades as you escape around the globe

oh sweet sailor traveler voyager harvester of hollow promise
i'd only myself to contend with and til now had forgone all truth
who are you what do you seek with your flimsy excuses

alone in my unhappiness with no one to share my burden
loser I who gave you so much was it not fill enough?
what am i what do i do what do i want i love you madly madness madness
transferred if your pain were as great i would surely die adieu
sacrifice ingratitude lose adieu i have surely not loved you enough
fuck me til i see the light once more oh empty page
oh boring repetition adieu begone i lie begone would that we had never met
i lie i die of grief not yet a poor crazed creature sane before we touched
adieu mourn for me for the lost tranquility i now despise another year adieu

the moment grows.

fifth letter

take the portrait the bracelets the letters (i will keep but 2 to remind me) you win i am convinced you don't love i won't love fini c'est fini i should have destroyed them all but they're yours have them back tokens they serve only to reinforce my own passion which i have become so attached to not you oh not you the spell you cast is broken the clouds over my eyes are gone

from *Flying Home*

FLYING HOME

i am flying home
catch me when i get there
the clouds increase in volume as i fly
decrease in volume   as i fly
night becomes day
day night

i am fond of music —
have my violin ready
sing me an aria

call to me later
when i reach the limits of your
voice.

ICARUS IN NO MAN'S LAND

in no man's land
in the middle of a field
on a blazing afternoon
pretty young girls
vie for the attention of a smoldering corpse

they have been told
he is a rich young handsome
man.

MIRRORS

this is not something
that has
memory

it is one small reflection
in a landslide
of
MIRRORS

SOLO

if there were only one star. one star. one man.

REST

there is no rest for one who is waiting. captured by waiting. always waiting.
my smile & rifle
always ready. my hands, full with waiting.

i am a creature of habit
i get so angry
i could burn down the world
i am not good at small talk

rest. i am always waiting to rest.

TRENCH PATROL

my job was going
from one trench to the
other
all the trenches were
interconnected
at spaced intervals
there were entrances
into the bunkers

always felt safest
underground

the taste of clouds
usually went away
as soon as there was a heavy
shelling
then all i could taste was my own sweat
& fear

    i longed to be a migrating bird
so i could taste the clouds   once again.

SOMME
(I CARRY YOU NO LONGER)

thin slight sickly man
i pray for you
i bless you
i wash my hands of you
i bless you
i pray for you
i wash my hands of you

virile servant
trapped within the fire of national anthem &
myth
i soak my cheeks in your forgetfulness
killer & killed

i wash my hands of you.

CRUNCH

at night i'm sacred i can't see anything left alone like a fish in a puddle i haven't killed anyone yet i'm special though i've got this staff in my hand & i smoke the best cigarettes that's what happens when you have pull even at the front I live like a king . . .

FRENCH POESIE

the green seaside
is in the corner of a room
where negatives
begin —
giant tableau
squashed into a bloodless evening

quietude
translating the scenery
transferring the image
to me
        become stiff & stark within the shifting
fertile nakedness

STOP DREAMING & CONCENTRATE

THE BIG ANGEL

it kills you while it's giving you life. i've been following my ashes for years. the Big Angel leads the way. i'll know it's spring when the corn starts growing & the grey of my hair starts melting again. though a land animal this angel follows the birds to their nests & tears out their feathers in bunches.

STRETCHED

from star to star
window to window
space to space
door to door
fragments of body
that contain the spirit
the tar from which we spring

oh fragility of flesh
blood dries inside the eye

& vanishes without
a trace

the tides swim within us

it is said that
we are mostly made
of water

DOOR

the door to his insides
                    opened like a canyon
                                        & the river that was
     his life flowed out
                         he hung suspended by the Sun's hand
       a ray of light
                    clinging to its own reflection.

TODAY

today my time has been wasted. again.
petty promises. false hoopla.
a possible change.
in my life.
in the direction of this war.
a chance that there will be no rain.

these bodies i step over will never know the difference.

         (i read your letter over & over again
but today i did not bring it with me)

         PEACE like shrapnel is just another fragment of WAR.

MIDNIGHT/NOON — the insomnia poems

(a series of poems dedicated to the Insomnia Drawings of Louise Bourgeois wherein 17 poems do hereby represent 220 drawings...... something for one to think about while lying awake at night.....)

"i love you because you make me feel good."
— L.B. from the Insomnia Drawings

for the person who has everything & wants more........ try insomnia

1.

stuck in geometry & its antecedents
counting 6's
            clock (s)ticks   caught in repetition & sequence

i.e.   dripping water   the slight variance of sound

each drop minutely painfully different than the next   music of holes

descend   within the 6's.

2.

red   a color i have aspired   to be made of
but not covered in

in winter i will lie with a big white lily
beneath the blankets
close to my chest
& a red mum on the pillow
beside my head

3.

lying here in bed   shackled to my fatigue waiting for the phonecall
that will eventually come   then your voice

4.

i'm not good @ small talk
i have so much anger i could burn up the world

the pillow extends to the river
the velvet reflects all shiny & red
within the trumpets' bells

they are lined up & lined w/gold
like the sounds names make
as they are extended into the river
wade a bit
then drop to the bottom
toward the mud
the water will extinguish the flame.

5.

blue as the light fell blue as the night fell blue as the light fell blue

pardon this   pause   yawn   eyesting

into the once upon   into the gone   into the i recall   into the blue

on the fine line within the fine line   pause yawn into the once upon into the gone.

6.

the brevity of sleep

fell asleep for a briefness
dreamt 2 duelists to the death
scored & scored each other's flesh
til only bone remained
one had a wooden leg
& even there the other
sliced & splintered to the marrow meat revealed red 'came sad inside.

7.

it was 4 o'clock in the morning
& all of a sudden the olives started talking really loud.

you know the green kind
with the rich red pimento
center.

8.

i cried for my newly dead friend
in my dream
i cried because there was nothing left to
say

my crying woke me up
& this was proof enough that i had finally
fallen asleep.

(if robert died that means he's dead.)

9.

the branches become snakes
the knife blades   fire
the bristles of the brush become match tips

hanging
things always
hanging

10.

i close my eyes like a book that i am too tired to read
a tune plays itself in my head
over & over again
as if it needed to get to know me

my eyes, that is,
open by themselves,
but thru the long & uneventful night remain unread.

11.

i tried to count buttons
the seeds from a sunflower
the circle formed by 2 lovers
kissing & when i fell for an instance
i dreamt of an ailing poet
playing a trombone

12.

looked for myself beneath the magnifying glass
within the whiteness of sleep
i looked for the seasons
& captured spring

i longed for myself
without getting up to pee
without yawning or working or watching the late nite news
& what i found & what i felt were the springs of the mattress
digging into my ribcage & hip.

13.

no wind
3:24 a.m.
i can tell by the cough
it's a man.

4 a.m.
i feel like the medicated dog of a famous author
as she rubs my stomach.

14.

insomnia is mostly circular
then lines & waves   like the passage of time   or the flowers of trees
the bedding down of bodies embraced & betrayed by life & myth

interlocking mounds of dust   portraits of hanged skin & geometry's
profiles of water   a dilating compass   the crisscross & nearmiss
of river & ocean   of tide & shore

elevated above the treeline there is a winding road   i am there somewhere
patches of moist hrs devour the clock as they gnaw at me

it is a continuous loop   well traveled
& i am always so tired

15.

sometimes i can only imagine my body
one small reflection in a landslide of mirrors

16.

this rain has ruined the roses
it is a continuous loop we travel
so tired
insomnia's a circle & we can only imagine the bodies of others
the woman in the moon is lost
& as i went looking for her last night
my branch began to blossom
but this rain's left no room for the roses
& spring never really arrived.

17.

the voice of the bird
is stuck somewhere between 5&6 in the morning
it is thick with notes
it opens suddenly & just as suddenly
falls silent
i am the only one awake to hear it
the dangerous hrs are between midnite & noon
it is here that i have nowhere to go
i am not safe even in my own bed
what i fear most is rejection & death
the bird having had a bad dream
woke for an instant
then fell mute then fell back to sleep
realizing it was still too early to share morning

where is the bird?

the one who is responsible for the salvation of a handful of cripples.
i will write my will when i write it
i am willing to do this
to be the one responsible for saving a handful of cripples
where is he?
how were so many of us fooled?

i am stuck between the ticks of the clock   counting 6's   24 is a safe # for some

— all poems written 2003

from *Saint Lucie*

st. lucy @ the opera   (life on its own terms)

1.
Life's a big place or so i think
& "the river deepens when it gets down to the sea"
i hold my eyes on a plate
& hold up the world for an instant
this is beauty in the ugliest sense
& not some would be pretender-to-the-throne
just trying to be grotesquely glamorous

Life's a big place
as i discovered just yesterday
& only sick people work in hospitals
& poetry like urine flow comes in streams
& sometimes you strain
& sometimes you don't
& sometimes you start
& sometimes you stop & then sometimes
you start
again
sometimes you empty your bladder all at once
only to discover moments later
it was not fully emptied
& sometimes there's the sensation
of not having emptied completely
this can be referred to as incomplete emptying
frequency
intermittency
urgency
weak stream
straining noctura

in the evening i carry my eyes into the world
& am met by frequent sometimes urgent looks
sometimes looks of longing & lust
& sometimes looks of love &
hate
i am blind so what i cannot see cannot hurt
me & what my eyes see they no longer
share   poet is a four letter word   like love & lust &
fuck & hate & kill

Life is a big Place & sometimes the weather
determines my day
i can't believe that i'm so naïve as to think that
by plucking out my eyes
men would no longer desire me
i can't believe that i'd ever say out loud that i'm
ashamed to be a human being
i can't believe i'd ever step into a subway car
on a cold & lovely eve
& there find a young & seemingly gentle &
handsome man
who offers to read me the signs
yes read them to me   i say
first he reads a poem of spring & then he reads
that if ever i see anything suspicious
i should call the terrorism HOTLINE
that's 1-800-T-E-R-R-O-R-I-S-M
that's unlikely   i say
& my heart's tongue whispers
read them to me again   for LIFE
is a Big Place
& since i am blind
& since i cannot see i cannot really say for sure i've
ever seen these things before
oh
you may hold my plate for awhile

if you like

Life's A BIG place
& in this room without gravity
the clock tells us how much sunlight
an umbrella holds
weight is heavier than it seems
& my eyes grow sleepy

art is more important than man
it is our footprint
it reminds us we've been here
but even art remains only for as long as we allow it
hurricane   flood   fire & MAN

my eyes grow sleepy in their chambers
& in the chamber that is my mouth
there remains a dry line
where the ocean has receded
a picture of memory's movement
a stranded swimmer
after hrs my mouth opens
to expel the wind
that has been locked there like a
strongman's grip
unable to lift itself
or balance itself in accordance with the law
what is the law?
a rundown clock that barely gives the time
but somehow makes me feel that i've only just
arrived?
a wind that falls like stone
onto the swimmer's feet after a long day
of laps?
what is the law?
the circling breath of a man
caught within a gravityless euphoria
heavy as a shadow that taps a melody as soundless

as a sunlit umbrella
on the concrete of a distant star?
rewinding the camera
without exposing the film?
winding the old victrola &
playing one's favorite tune?
not to kiss me if you are married?
not to flirt with greed
unless it means a meal ticket?
not to catch sunlight in your umbrella
but if you do please let it go
or save some for a time when the weather
might determine your day?
i must be falling in love
can i have my plate back now?

it takes the clock forever to move just minutes
in this room without gravity
it is stuck somewhere between time &
breath
this space i am in
feels a bit like being trapped within the petals
of the ranunculus
its folds enfolding me
& in its center lies a weightlessness
heavy as a star

i open my mouth to walk
& the timeline that is me rattles
like a tin can or a bell
i fall
i cough
i swallow doorknobs
& open the sounds that crawl inside my belly
my mouth grabs itself like an inhaling balloon
as i try unlocking the 1st gate

LIFE is a BIG PLACE

what is the law?
to stay afloat on this island for as long as i can
& never forget i'm in space
this is beauty in the ugliest sense

but now i will lift my eyes
& listen more closely to the OPERA
& never end singing with a
SONG

2.
what is opera?

COMPOSER & LIBRETTIST
OVERTURE & FINALE
ARIA CHORUS & DUET

where are the words when we need them? trapped inside a mouth
like a draught in the ocean
& if the opera is a success we thank the composer
& if the opera is a flop we blame the libretto

— 5/02/03, from fragments written 4/03

back 1-4 (Matisse)

1.

i looked for you
all day
at the museum
&
for better or
worse
you were nowhere
to
be
found.

2.

i thought
art
would help
reconcile
us
instead it's
driven
us
further a
part.

3. (monet's water lilies)

it's not how
it
looked to him
but how
he interpreted it

transformed it
into his own
language
while processing
distilling
&
creating
that
language.

4.

bare
unbroken
then
emancipated
the focus
sliding
off
my
backbone.

* my backbone *can be substituted for* her backbone

from *Invisible Ray*

temporary respite wind flowers/fung wah

(water creatures reprise) 3/17/05, bus to boston, & 3/18/05, nyc

a.

boxcars on either side of the tollbooth
bumpy ride for wind flowers
tho in wind undulation is not like a slow motion cartoon

there is gentle & then there is the standard
the moat that protects us from ourselves

proof that water exists
that we are not gentle equipment   as time moves us

that we are indeed, in some meta-sense,
made of NUTS & BOLTS

that the arches that form our bodies
are being constantly re-invented

that lots are drawn way in advance
as some of us indeed move into the category of antique
our ABCs more or less intact but
expressed
shaped   slightly different

what i hope for is that tables remain on time
what i expect are more delays

hunts & stabs at. . . . .
                                        ham longings diminished
laws & sections of laws re-interpreted

that the one way is many-fold
that ologies & nologies are reformed reliably
yet manifest

RU ACH HA KODESH **RU ACH HA KO DESH**

bare are these days so full with playing fields

light a new haven in these overcast days of angels

ru ach ha ko desh (*whispered)*

yes — i love angels too
they defy thruways
their linen wings outstretching like yawns
their things neatly folded in a corner
outsmarting the coroner always

LOVE is still a funny word that holds a KEY
as keys open cracks in the cracked field
defrosting the pond

new latent pelts reform our skins
& we are never belonging
never home
must never forget
we are quiet emergency
alcohol & smoke
must never forget
we are driver & driven
mask & sea & land
on the way to delay without delay
a short break within the breaks
god's breath on water
moot & mote

must never forget we are luggage litter cracks
bag gage

litter   cracks   lug gage   litter   light   clean
bare-branched budding thinkers
squawkers   cry babies
I-pods & seminal fluids made whole
cellmates & cell phone phreaks
blank screens that will never reach 100
carpeting on the roof of the father's mouth

boxcars on either side of the tollbooth

water creatures swimming in the flag/furling CON
of the green smothered Lane
in a green steepled whirl

i have become part of this EARTH
a glass half empty
the perfect Host   (until next week's rush)
a forum for   medicine
water & gate
                PASS   THRU   ME   pass thru me

RU ACH HA KODESH ru ach ha kodesh   god's breath on water   pass thru me

b.

kill me in 4's   on all fours
here it is bogey woman   in time in
"open time"
here it's straight as a popsicle before the meltdown
                a NEW CENTURY
possessive of many qualities of the old . . . . STOP
STOP. . . . . collecting destinies   exits . . . .
  super highways not so super anymore

again the need to reinvent things
fresh linens
wrinkled train ties
poetically sculptured electrical poles

wire upon wire
glass & mirror   plastic phenomenon
prime sources   fat spring   faculties
econology   reliable stores   the bindings of books

crack the book in 2   sew the book is always open

closed book that keeps the daylight out   light in
oh rider   ease down
super   super   work my bone golden angel

paradise: skymiles   palm trees   & gentle breezes
stars too numerous to name

we brick & bricked up enterprises   glass mirror plastic phenomenon
truth be told this truth be told
JEHOVAH filled with passion & shaken
tots be ester   knew   i   think   hum   us   hum   us
rising high to touch   bum us   sum   us
explain us to ourselves
we locals   be local

YOU ARE HERE — safety off   a better day   wil.........l......
more or less   in dust (t)ria(i)l(s)   stone & steel
bridges
poetically sculpted   thig-a-ma-jigs....   Sang
&   sang........
the only **HITCH**   is........................never.

language is an organism

1.

bundle of information
parody of nerves / brains / residue / residuals

i am a survivor of language
host to language seeds
& social interaction
we are cohorts (the final)
conductors
a new language of complex codes
little inconsistencies
heads / biologies
we all don't end up with the same language
language makes us human / we all don't end . . . UP
language grows inside us . . . stimulus
nice way to do things / establish an order / borrowing uncomplicated sentences

x amount of time for x amount of crime / tapped out of self within a neutral space
an inf(l)ection / special modulations / finely marked / given / received
@ the end of the pointing the dialect produced the color of one's clothing
& respect for one's shirt
pushing one's link into a neutral space / producing co-reference
lin(k)ed up & shot / this is when the storm happens
when the new form is forming

2.

stimulus — nice ways to do things — establish an order —
a nominal output of here-within
natural se(l)ection —
a missing idea
how our traits are passed down / how to throw an inheritance
to bury an eco-system — destroy & reproduce our learning processes
inferred genes / implanted communications excised from our brains

emerging / submerging / extending the GAP
exposing / describing the SIGNS > the turns within the system
sorting the trees along the pathway / the highway / the trail that leads to MAN
who goes no WHERE / which leads NO where

it's like > time travelling within a 3D SpAcE.

from *Fool's Gold*

mariposa

there is no need for debt or debate
when one does not mean anything to anybody
the important point is not to break the chain
to be polite — to say yes & thank you
to be accommodating — to supplement even supplant
desires — to persist — consomenations /
irritated whites drinking Negronis
ah butterfly the nemesis is you — short life spans colliding
perhaps all life changing as you change
encounter & encompass grief — hear the flutter of 100,000
the sonic tracks of a silent film
the debt converted to smoke
windows clouded over
city spitting clouds
that wedge
between the arches
of her
high heeled shoes

i said i'm no longer afraid to look

shuttered windows — der wekstahlvez
paper blowing across an empty street
debt or depth or death
which is it — all fool's gold
no matter what the substance
all duped no matter what the price.
werder da cat's on its quiet pursuit
the unrest of pigeons
as the prison gates open & you are released like a steam engine
into the street — released from your oustem —
& we walk like comrades & i pour the morning's waste out of a bucket

as the crowd increases from single file to tenfold
rows up & down pathways / cobbles cabals cables
stairways & staring soldiers marching
the organ grinder playing
the draw bridge near collapse
ah mariposa
the factory awaits its occupants — what is the debt they owe
we owe? — heya-ah heya-ah heya-ah

a pipe — a moustache — the gears beginning to spin
in a world of mass production
where things are produced for the masses
though some are only for the privileged few
finely shaved & polished shards of steel
infinite bottles filled & loaves fresh baked
fires stoked
chimneys pushcarts / loaded
cars washed — garbage disposed of
(yet always more garbage) — days always beginning
children off to school if the season's right
weggelerollerda window gates up schlachterha — mer
curtains up
blinds up — mannequins — horses — up — pillows aired — blinders on
rugs beaten — butterflies remembering what they were then forgetting
just as quickly — shoes shined — nails polished
a beautiful walk thru the park at night
the band playing — the globe changing (color)
junkies all quietly tucked away somewhere
dancers as graceful as flowers
crack one legged crutch man
no stories about war or war stories
just elevator rides and roll-top desks
typewriters telephones & the printing press
operator operator i am coming to the end of a tunnel
the light is beginning to spread
the evacuation of the dirt that is my heart is in full swing
at all other times i will dial 311
the barber smiles

the sound of lighting a cigarette on a singing man's knee
like achtspracht breathing
no debt no debate — grief for the moment everlasting

fly away mariposa — away your colorful wings
the naked children are here only to exploit you
            to explore you
        to touch your fascinating wings —
it was even shorter than anticipated — a quick beautiful twin burst
    too short & me preoccupied with 3 different lives
        & she flew torn & traumatized she flew
but cacophony calculation dark spectrum debt ceiling & me indebted to few men
    heart strumming — cycles — disposing of the evening's waste
one stage is flying great distances to approach the indecipherable
    travelling lord i'm travelling tryin to make heaven my home
 rocks — next — i can't begin to tell you how it looks from where i sit
            lamp trim & burning
  end time   dream time
      indecipherable redness that reflects an obvious exit
            desperation on every corner
      i can't begin to tell you mariposa — even from here
      in this parking lot there is a history of butterflies
            guns money jelly rolls
    just as there is a history of lost pages — gaps in memory
        always lost here in this same cocoon
            there is for me @ any rate
      the mystery of a smile & why it occurs or when
       in all these photographs i look so pensive
           angry, disturbed but rarely smiling — all bare knuckled
            & @ the end i must shed my cocoon
        in a tunnel without end where depth & ceiling are one
           as they press in upon me —
nemesis — is me oh butterfly — coal dust — the price i put on things
 & i can't begin to tell you where it all began
   but look there & there & there & there
      & you'll begin to see the end.

from *As Collage*

for Emily Dickinson

here is fascical knowledge
the pin plus pen
a fragment enveloped within shifting
influences (*this segment of the poem is dedicated*
to a woman who wrote along the edges
of envelopes)
the falling apart of structure
the shortage of elements
the how of war & its collapses
& how it collapses / eclipses our desires
fragments us like explosions
divides us into temporal new wholes
coughing horrors OF (-s)
changing sentinels that (re)g(u)ard our words
as we guard our words
& are sentenced to hiding

we change our identities the way
we change our penmanship
the way unnamed manuscripts are lost
illegible or in eternal transition
internal rotation
a carnival of facsimiles
like history —
the falling apart from structure
gesture / inscription / legible to
illegible / landmarked temporality of
souls / dissected / hammered / nailed to the wall

is falling a part of structure?

(*think of this portion as being in the shape of an envelope*)

silence

there is nothing left to say
sitting here at the edge of the world
surrounded by emptiness & all
that it contains —
but this thinking
this idea of thinking — of words — language
communication just won't stop
outside the war has stopped for the moment
inside it never stops
somewhere there is peace for the moment
inside there never is
my head is pounding —
outside the explosions have stopped
for the moment
but inside they never stop
outside the world becomes silent for the moment
the silence presses in around me
deafens me >
then explodes inside my head
my thoughts have stopped for the moment
& i am at peace finally at peace
though the one thing that can never be
is . . .

— 11/23–26/14

sunset poems

THE RAIN HAS STOPPED FOR US TODAY
THE SUN COMES OUT AT SUNSET
THE WIND BRAYS SWEETLY THRU THE NOW PALE ONION FLOWERS
OPEN TO A NEW DIVERSITY
THE SOUNDS OF EQUIVALENCE   AND RHYME

BUT IT IS STILL AND ALWAYS WILL BE TRUE
THAT COLUMBUS   NEVER STOPPED HERE

incomplete sunset

it's too cold by the river
i came here unexpectedly i am not
properly dressed
i can barely see what's in front
of my face
from staring into the sun
too long
i move south with it
to get as clear a view as possible
as it sets
near the end it is hidden by clouds
some nice things happen but the sun itself is lost
i am shivering   the sunset is incomplete
i am incomplete this poem   incomplete

marred sunset

though marred by clouds
there is this spectacular burst of light
as the sun recedes behind the architecture
i'm sure some of my circuits were burnt out back then
just too much I want to learn/do

& so little capacity to do it all
in the true intellectual set
my own architecture marred by too much light

the kid's a quiet emotional wreck
as we discuss sunset songs on sunset boulevard
monsters with two heads
& acts of desperation
both existential & class related

i write prose all the time
like which kid? me or him?
get a haircut.
don't never get a haircut i want to tell him
& yes   it's always better on the big screen
even the small flat screen
in an ever diminishing room
will never suffice

serenity
& the burst is over as fast as it occurs
the water is slightly undulating
though i am not calm
all around me seems to be so
the water filling up my bladder once again
within such a short period of time
voices coming from the yacht
midway out on the water
stop as quickly as they start
laughter being barely audible

i pick up a stick of unused gum
still in its foil wrapper
& place it on a bench

i chose to hear the sunset tonight
rather than watch the music
she tells me i'm a writer   the squeaky pier

as i long for true madness to descend upon me
like a sudden burst of light
& finally bring clarity to my stained
stagnant mind
& quickly finish me off

i'm so hopelessly trapped inside this fence
as
i whisper good night to the
strangling rope.

— hudson river, 5/16/16

sunset for Oscar Wilde

perhaps my fascination with sunsets is over
i have come to realize that
like with most other obsessions
i will never be satisfied with what i get
like the lecture where no matter how great you were
& how much you gave @ the end — no one had any questions
when what you were looking forward to most was the Q & A

would you rather have someone who does
THIS in this situation or this in THIS situation
but due to the fact that you were watching remnants of a sunset
you never quite got to figure out what THIS or this actually were

it's a hot summer night with a perfect breeze ruffling the waves
which create that quiet wave murmur
"& THIS / this evening is just like any other evening" —
the gulls must be thinking
as they glide slowly to their perches
& into slumber.

"Art creates an incomparable and unique effect, and, having done so, passes on to other things. Nature, upon the other hand, forgetting that imitation can be made the sincerest form of insult, keeps on repeating this effect until we all become absolutely wearied of it. Nobody of any real culture, for instance, ever talks nowadays about the beauty of a sunset. Sunsets are quite old-fashioned. They belong to the time when Turner was the last note in art. To admire them is a distinct sign of provincialism of temperament. Upon the other hand they go on. Yesterday evening Mrs. Arundel insisted on my going to the window, and looking at the glorious sky, as she called it. Of course I had to look at it. She is one of those absurdly pretty Philistines to whom one can deny nothing. And what was it? It was simply a very second-rate Turner, a Turner of a bad period, with all the painter's worst faults exaggerated and over-emphasised."

— Oscar Wilde, from "The Decay of Lying: an Observation" (1889)

bird poems

ice floe
sea birds
bobbing

---

morning haze:
only birds & cherry blossoms
awakened

---

thru her breathing   birdsong

---

an old woman feeds old birds
i try to get her attention

i am nearing a point of hunger
i feel honest & ridiculous
my stomach fills with morning birds

---

the left-handed bird

as a man i am left-handed
as a bird i'd be left-winged
they say all lefties have genius
but i do not believe them
they cannot all be liars
yet i still do not believe them

i will neither alter history
become history
or change history

i will not worship at altars
& will not buy new clothing
i'll find my own solutions
& will not fault the layman

i will not bask in glory
& won't become a hero
my name will not be spoken
my words will not be judged
i will not be part of history
i will not spread revolution

---

sparrows seem aggressive

she says the sparrows
swoop in groups she says
they are longer thinner than
American sparrows & hang in a
line as they chatter
the brothers hang side by side
on the wall
friendship is a long thin
portrait of trial, error & love.

— paris

---

the birds begin to swoop / scatter
there is the singularity of one voice

"singing"
nothing else
the clouds & their doubles
the endless stream of birds
rising out of the river

— toulouse

---

sunset
rising out of the river
an endless stream

of birds

---

cemetery

in a landscape of mildew & stone
a bird watches me
mocks me like the buffoon that i am
i know it is there somewhere
already eaten by a cat   it mocks me
& sings to me from the belly
then becomes shit
& seeps into the mud
to be song again

— père lachaise, paris

tree haiku

the little boy
shooting trees
with his new toy gun

heavy rains &
over night
cherry blossoms

sudden thunder —
cherry blossoms
shiver

hana gu mori — (flower clouds)
camellia blossom rests
in the buddha's lap

red pine or cherry blossoms
which do you
prefer?

morning haze
only birds & cherry blossoms
awakened

eating sweets &
watching cherry blossoms
is like a handshake

the sound of a life saver
against my teeth
cherry blossoms

yesterday hot
today cold
the ginkgo so confused

gentrification —
outside my door
the blossoming pear tree

children's magical garden / white autumn

the flower of days —
a meditative stretch tattooed
to the eyes
numbered up
where the blue is religion
where the thin veins are green figured
shadows
on tightened yellow sunlight
prettier than convulsion /

marking the vacant windows' history
tattered shades
½ drawn
a catty-cornered view of both sides of loneliness

i can't help wanting to fill the empty blackboard
with all these human thoughts confined
or *picked up by the breeze*

autumn has finally arrived — even these empty chairs sense this
a definitive act
voodoo stick & wheelbarrows
re-animating the near dead wall sense this
the blanketed children sense this
the soil senses this so too the dog

the flower need not be painted over just repainted in spots

WELCOME
It's Open

it's a beautiful day
even if it's a bit behind schedule
it's a cool beautiful autumn-kind-of-day.

— *9/24/16*

Bruce Nauman

contrapposto studies, i through vii

(i've forgotten the order in which i've written this — the first the last the last the first)

i. as *you quietly implode*
your glasses somewhere snug in your shirt pocket
sometimes — this **I** *i feel is going backward*
me *or your body*
(de) shaped *so we begin again @ the end of some*
young horse breeders search before (non) elasticity &
horses *as even the room empties into itself*
this joint (your joints) heavily disjointed
& you are left with(out) your nakedness — the turnabout & its blankness
a wall of blank scratches black & white inverted
a positive (un) colliding with its negative *(SO tell ME) — what's NEW?*
gravel-pit sound your innards (BELLY BELIES) your steps making
under that t-shirt — what is that box under your t-shirt
those gurgle-like sounds your belly is making
your occasional *YAH YAAAAHHHHH* *isolated YAH yah —* ***GOT IT****?*

ii. miked & holding tight to the base of your skull

iii. motion in
motion & contrary to
itself *BEHIND the FALSE* PARTITION
negation of the positive "LOOP"

black white becoming each other there is a known NO — difference
quantum flatness (makes)

becoming themselves — "difficult to watch" — the *NY TIMES* intones
child's play's all's i see by an aging man recalling his own-ness or

regretting it — replaying it different for his camera as it has aged
along with him —
difficult NO *in parts or as a whole* IM*/parts —*
old is the re-examiner re-examining his own history
presenting the past as it is now into its (one's) OWN HIS *story*
un gracefully swimmer-ing of a concrete mixer & how he was-is-n't
a mixed & mixed up money horse dealing layerer

iv. ***RE*** *-*
validate
concurrent with emergence sees obsess
touch nose · or bypass it
TURN (A) ROUND
la ronde around
cubistic in its own abstracting way
then quickly scratch your nose
now place YOU *beside a wall of outlets & nails*
then turn
U Turn nRuT U as the studio remains so ***STILL***
yet still it moves unknowingly —
what lies under the folds of your shirt that moves you
so like life-hardening jello?

insect hola as it begats theirself

v. step toe (as a dancer might)

sequence as non-sequential as obvious order — behind your head hands exploding
you are thinking — ***YES***? *pensive — disparaged — disposed / of*

we are divided amongst my selves
this is something illness brings
can bring
generic illness
specific illness
now flat screen works with heads behind
your tail wiggle twist
katydids drowning shortly in their own piss

(in philadelphia the story as different as it is the same) —
i'd rather be

vi. subtext: *how the body inhabits itself*
inhibits itself
rejects its self
unglues itself then puts its selves back together
at times rather haphazardly
always squaring off swearing off / avoiding while *colliding*

how we are / it is / can be / presented in other contexts
(again in re(e)ality in philly)
with smaller versions of our selves
as in this case as in MOCK UPS as in MOCK ME as in **I MOCK ME**

vii.
your glasses disappear from your pocket
there are holes beneath your armpits
your skin leaks out of your t-shirt
your black is white
your flesh is x-ray —

we are (I) separated from the OTHER as sure as we are ONE
in movement — the crypt will open to illness
the grave(l) pit sound of impending LIFE & how it overlaps
with the / un \ known — KNOWN in 7 parts of reversal
the many fold way of front backwards from bottom's up (WARD) of . . .

— Bruce Nauman at sperone westwater, October 2016

the death of america

here's to the death of America   of sequins & high heals
formless & unformed trumpets   & strumpets & triumphs
here's to the death of America here's to plutocracy oligarchy & freedom
here's to the death of progress to the air we carry with us
here's to a life of Barbie doll family values

when our humanity is taken from us   we only have our humanity to rely on
here's to our humanity   let's take back our humanity
in order to retrieve what has been taken from us
let us question our humanity as we reclaim it
repossess it / rotten / over-ripened consumerism
our freedoms are being robbed
our identities called into question here's to the death of America
to you America and your demise to the robots we've become

here's to that virus called promise and change
that so many cling to / here's to the "Judas calf"
to the continuance of dialogue or its demise
here's to our loss of autonomy should we completely lose our way
here's to the autonomy we've already lost but either don't see it
choose not to see it or worse yet choose to accept it

here's to bloody bloodless revolutions to power structures & hierarchies
here's to anarchy   where is anarchy? here's to the bad guys   who are the bad guys?
where are the bad guys who uses real bullets? obsessed with power and control
we are all obsessed with power & control

can we really work with the regime without totally going mad? while still in chains?
all those chain smoking coal-miners-to-be in chains   those mind boggling chains

here's to awakening & to seeing our world for what it is

here's to censorship & to upending the balance of power
to roleplaying in this complicated maze
here's to lying in wait at the center of promises

& waiting for those promises to be broken closely without going mad going mad
over the death of America over one's personal shame

there's a chill down the spine a collective chill for many
it's called the peaceful transition of power
not   "look — they now seem to like each other"
it's called democracy not like in a total totalitarian system
where one guy just kills the other then seizes power
in this case it's just kill her with bad constitutional ideals
it's called one wants to literally capitalize from the other's booty
our so-called floundering fathers were slave owners conmen & murderers
despite what good intentions some of them had

psssst there's something i need to tell
there's something happening here America is dying
america can never be what we were told it could be
but listen carefully it can be worse a lot worse

America is dying but hopefully a new America will be resurrected
through its death & begin to live yet again the death of America

— November 9 onward, 2016

(some language in this poem taken from a village voice article dated nov 2–nov 8 written about the HBO show Westworld)

from *Black Magic*

syracuse, or the panther-man

I spit

the orange taxi got it out roasted cool COFFEE you Took advantage opposite simple think setback honeycomb stenographers lack absolutely modern hygiene morality with Colleen bread vertically yellow bronze pneumatic daily political man addressed the young slave in elevator Marie Antoinette negro savings bank beehive foodstuffs Dr. Mutual Dr. Hot chocolate beard the only food to feed reasoning animals facts I am a realist tradition trade union fire lynching was a frequent amusement.

Fist shaking from a distance.

We were never spoken load special talk today our sentimental whining and philanthropic kitty our misfortunes uncle Tom's cabin colonization segregation individual liberty here here the hours pass for an by ourselves* Spinal banner dog Camaro concealed from you loan to the pass Emerson Roosevelt metropolis not Tim buck too . . . external shut his largemouth Black is the depths of the loudspeaker:

BLACK MAGIC

Don't believe in chains don't tell lies don't neglect your wives and children don't forget where you live don't settle your quarrels with the razor don't carry flash of liquor in your pockets don't shoot it ghosts Believe in progress flags the Knights of Samson the grand parade.

Nomad shepherd nimble nimble blue oval class nimble on Monday night low road confidence opposing forces straddling continents language Financial oligarchy proletariat sunrise of deliverance what 1789 did for that joo what 1917 did for the workers revolution Gold laced grabber penetrated by Earth only well Sacco and Vanzetti I spit on the white man's gift Africa 500 years ahead of I'm at goosy conviction have nothing more compact hyena there can be nothing.

Underdog everywhere wearing his Gentile frock coat birth of the world leaning in restful scent moldings weapons savagery Rights sepia blood red landscapes of this attorney quiet tone frescoes Congo dance grandfather's lane the thread reappeared autumnal floods with no pool no ruins the land like America two new (nude) savages.

The old question was taken up again . . . the old skin

S lashes of the tiger borrowed from see and forest creatures eyes modeling deep and cool like cave hot shutter the songs he new at home spontaneously reverting to the terror of wild beasts salmons crocodile skin guitars calabash Women weeping in this that last sleep the narrow sarcophagi the News without paddles by factories Bear cross he crossed the section of masks the symbols of secret societies Blue black-and-white Anthony patterns tattooing shoulder gratitude very truth magnetic regions fruit trees Game hunters wild beast triple crest clan comical monstrous hollow war drums the whole museum.

Flint spearheads rusty nails since the trappings Magic ambulance ambulets imprisoned Foods is an illusion come back in The name of the spirit.

Bluz made an empty space around themselves. typed> (the Blooms)

Vamp Joy in living red figures his will his strength new being humane corrective graph mal efficient staying spilled ink Clay shadow touched his body sign into close longspine Brown spots frock coat simultaneously thundered out vicious in his flying flank . . .

Cry right now klores custodians bellowing.

lace

(the music of Zeena Parkins)

quartet for the child that's got its own

i look at my watch / it is 9:11
tonite the date is 9/11
it's time for the quartet to end as 3 to become
tell 'em willie boy was is . . .
lace like for jeremy's heavy shoes / in 5 movements
she is a child blessed / no less than any other
she is in 5 movements / is the maker of lace
is 6 branches / their leaves artificial
but when they produce wind the room subtly shakes

i am truly left handed
this is evident by the way i write
my wrist in an awkward painful curve
laced / but not quite the memory
i'd like to remember / now all memories hurt
i am waiting to die & be insurrected

he sits silently on the other side of the glass
where i know the music reaches him
the room is on full tilt
the glass looks both ways
man is as man does
woman is . . . a school for higher learning
who are these gadgets?
blips on a computer screen
recording for posterity
tangible endgames deflected by LACE / drapery
he comes through all his adversities
awaiting signals from the glass
walking on the other side of the room
more than a presence & red lights of traffic's
movement as eye is glued to camera

movement inside its lens
she allows for space / egg on a table
lines falling where they may
as she untangles the threads the brass creates
moments are defined by each movement
& not the other way around.

— the stone, 9/11/19

SELECTED BIBLIOGRAPHY

People and *Places* (Bayonne, NJ: The Beehive Press, circa 1995)

Subway Assemblages (Arcadia, FL: JVC Books, 2000)

A Superintendent's Eyes (New London, CT: Hozomeen Press, 2000; Brooklyn: Unbearable Books/Autonomedia, 2013)

The Final Nite & Other Poems: Complete Notes from a Charles Gayle Notebook 1987–2006 (Brooklyn: Ugly Duckling Presse, 2006, 2024)

Logos and Language: A Post-Jazz Metaphorical Dialogue, with Matthew Shipp (Paris: RogueArt, 2008)

Reaching into the Unknown 1964–2009, with Jacques Bisceglia (Paris: RogueArt, 2009)

The Mantis for Cecil Taylor 1966–2009 (Island Heights, NJ: Iniquity Press/ Vendetta Books, 2009 and 2011)

Long Play, the complete Evan Parker poems (Rusden, UK: Corrupt Press, 2011)

As Collage, an unpublished series of 73 poems written in 2013–2015

Flying Home, with Sig Bang Schmidt (Paris: Paris Lit Up Press, 2015)

The Invisible Ray (Brooklyn: Overpass Books, 2016)

Black Magic (Oyster Bay, NY: New Feral Press, 2017)

Frozen Heatwave, with Yuko Otomo (Columbus, OH: Luna Bisonte Prods, 2017)

Where Night and Day Become One: The French Poems 1983–2017 (New York: Great Weather for Media, 2018)

be/ond seh flinges, with Jim Leftwich (Columbus, OH: Luna Bisonte Prods, 2020)

Vorstoßen ins Unbekannte. Poeme & Collagen, translated by Jürgen Schneider (Berlin: Hybriden-Verlag, 2021)

Tendant le bras vers l'Inconnu, translated by Franck Andrieux (Montpellier: L'Appeau Strophe, 2025)

www.ingramcontent.com/pod-product-compliance
Lightning Source LLC
LaVergne TN
LVHW091946301026
851422LV00028B/118